The Old Testament

by
William V. and Patricia R. Coleman

Twenty-Third Publications
P.O. Box 180
West Mystic, CT 06388

©Copyright 1978—Twenty-Third Publications

A Catechist's Prayer

Something new is happening, Lord,
    something different, untried, untested.
That something new is me,
    a me different from before,
    a me with more life lived,
        more pain endured,
        more joy imbibed.
This new me will try to share my life with the young.

They will call me teacher
    and expect marvels from me,
    hate me when I am right,
    despise me when I am wrong.
They will cut their adolescent teeth upon my sensitivities.
They will reject me and call me fool.
They will try to shock me with their unbelief,
    real or imagined.
They will, in turn, come to me with tears when belief fails them.
They will depend on me and hate me because of their dependence.
They will rejoice with me about themselves
    and never see that I, too, need to rejoice about myself.
They will use me,
    feed on me,
    grow from the substance of my life.
And, be unaware of it.

I cannot go this road alone, Lord,
I need to depend on someone, as they depend on me.
I need a sense of someone caring,
    someone helping,
    someone sharing the exuberance and the joy,
                      the pain and the humiliation.
I need a friend, just as they need one.
You are it, Lord, my friend.

Help me when the going is rough.
Rejoice with me when I feel I have the world at my feet.
Weep with me when my dreams shatter into tiny bits of crystal.
Above all, be with me as you were with Mary.
May I too be full of grace and blessed.
And may the fruit of my work be blessed, as He once was.

Amen, Lord. Amen.

                                              William V. Coleman

An Old Testament Prayer

Lord, may I reflect the greatness of those who have walked before me
  in this troubled land of ours.
May I listen to music of Your kingdom's song
  as it calls me to become what they have been,
  men and women of faith,
  people of courage,
  those who heard Your holy voice.

May I have that faith of Abraham,
  the courage to walk where You have called me,
  the strength to face a world which cannot understand,
  and the resolve to walk to my mountain of sacrifice wherever
    that may be.

May I seek true freedom as the wise Moses did.
  A freedom to raise my voice in sounds of praise.
  A freedom to become a people bound by love
    But anchored, too, in love's shadow—justice and its
      demanding law.

And may I be as independent as old Samuel,
  unwilling to submit to tyranny and power
    but rather to listen first to Your voice sounding in my
      inner heart,
  and to resist all those who by power or blandishment
    would take away the freedom You have given me.

May I have the sensitivity of young David,
  a clear compassion for my fellows in the land,
  a desire to lead them to a tryst with You,
  and a willingness to be misunderstood even by those
    who most of all should love me.

And finally, may I have the prophet's voice strong against injustice,
  with a hard and steely resolution to die
    before I submit to what degrades my fellow man,
  with a mind wise and open to new ways
  and with a heart willing to sense new thoughts about You
    and the life You have given me to live.

Lord, may I reflect the greatness of those who have walked before me
  in this troubled land of ours.
May I listen to the music of Your kingdom's song
  as it calls me to become what they have been,
    men and women of faith,
    people of courage,
    those who heard Your holy voice.

Amen, Lord. Amen.

(Duplicator master of this sheet in packet)

Contents

Part I/Introductory Material

A Catechist's Prayer.. 2
An Old Testament Prayer... 3
How to Use This Book.. 6
Ideas for Special People 7
Some Thoughts About Teenagers... 8
Our Theological Position 9
Content Analysis.. 10
Special Suggestions for This Volume 11
Planning Chart.. 12

Part 2/Lessons

1 **Abraham: Finding a God to Believe In** 15
   Catechist's Background
   Model Presentation
   Pondering Point
   Primary Lesson Plan (Task Sheet)
   Alternate Lesson Plan
   Mini Lessons
   Catechist Resource Sheet

2 **Free At Last** 31
   Catechist's Background
   Model Presentation
   Pondering Point
   Primary Lesson Plan (Task Sheet)
   Alternate Lesson Plan (Study Sheet)
   Mini Lessons

3 **Forming a People** 47
   Catechist's Background
   Model Presentation
   Pondering Point
   Primary Lesson Plan (Task Sheet)
   Alternate Lesson Plan
   Mini Lessons
   Catechist Resource Sheet

4 **The Lawgiver**... 63
   Catechist's Background
   Model Presentation
   Pondering Point
   Primary Lesson Plan (Task Sheet)
   Alternate Lesson Plan
   Mini Lessons
   Catechist Resource Sheet

5	**The Voice of Discontent**	79
	Catechist's Background	
	Model Presentation	
	Pondering Point	
	Primary Lesson Plan (Task Sheet)	
	Alternate Lesson Plan (Study Sheet)	
	Mini Lessons	
	Catechist Resource Sheet	
6	**The Voice of Practicality**	95
	Catechist's Background	
	Model Presentation	
	Pondering Point	
	Primary Lesson Plan (Task Sheet)	
	Alternate Lesson Plan	
	Mini Lessons	
	Catechist Resource Sheet	
7	**The Price of Faith**	109
	Catechist's Background	
	Model Presentation	
	Pondering Point	
	Primary Lesson Plan (Task Sheet)	
	Alternate Lesson Plan	
	Mini Lessons	
	Catechist Resource Sheet	
8	**Prophecy**	125
	Catechist's Background	
	Model Presentation	
	Pondering Point	
	Primary Lesson Plan (Task Sheet)	
	Alternate Lesson Plan	
	Mini Lessons	
	Catechist Resource Sheet	
9	**New Theologies**	139
	Catechist's Background	
	Model Presentation	
	Pondering Point	
	Primary Lesson Plan (Task Sheet)	
	Alternate Lesson Plan	
	Mini Lessons	
	Catechist Resource Sheet	
10	**The Recap**	155

Part 3/Experiential Living and Learning

An Old Testament Weekend 158

How to Use This Book

Probably nothing in the contemporary Church presents more difficulty than the catechesis of teenagers. Teachers blame the textbooks. Parents blame the teenagers. And, teenagers blame the teachers. Some parents believe the whole problem can be solved by returning to the old Baltimore Catechism. Some pastors are unwilling to admit the seriousness of the problem and retreat to plans for new organization or a new director of religious education.

This program makes no pretense of solving all that is wrong. The roots of the problem are entwined with the roots of the crises in contemporary culture, family life, and religion. All that the loyal catechist can hope to do is to present the message of Jesus in a reasonably attractive way and reinforce that message with his or her own personal faith. The Spirit of God can and will do the rest.

The purpose of this program then is to present the message in an attractive way, one that is both simple for the inexperienced teacher and challenging for the old hand in the classroom. This program can be used in any grade or grouping of grades from nine to twelve. This means that the teacher must adapt the material to the age level of the students. Experience has shown that this is an easy matter and one that must be done with any traditional text since students fail to meet publishers' schedules for maturation. With no text in the students' hands the task of adaptation is easier rather than more difficult.

The Lesson's Components

Each lesson begins with a section titled **Catechist's Background.** In these essays, the serious catechist will discover historical, theological and pedagogical material which will assist him or her in achieving a deeper understanding of the topic presented in the lesson. None of this material is to be presented to the students in the form found here but serves to enrich the catechist and to help sort out adult problems born of one's own catechesis.

In these background presentations, emphasis will be placed on the understandings and approaches of our own childhood and today's theological and catechetical thought. We have chosen to do this not to denigrate the old ways but to point out some of the profound changes that have taken place in Catholic teaching. Unless the catechist is aware of these changes, it will be difficult for him or her to approach some of the lessons without distorting them.

After the **Catechist's Background** essay is a **Model Presentation.** The purpose of this model is to guide the catechist in a class presentation. It is not expected that the catechist memorize it or read it to the class in its present form. Rather, the intent of the presentation is outlined at the beginning of the essay so that each catechist may make his or her own presentation following the points outlined there. This presentation is followed by a **Pondering Point,** a short thought for the catechist to ponder as he or she reflects on the material presented in the unit.

These three essays are followed by two distinct lesson plans. The first (the **Primary Plan**) is easier to use. It is based on small group discussion, a report to the class of these discussions, a discussion of these reports and a reflection by the catechist on the topic discussed.

The second (the **Alternate Plan**) may be used in addition to the first plan or in place of it. The activities are varied in this alternate plan but they, too, lead to a catechist's presentation based on the **Model Presentation.** When both the primary and the alternate plans are used, the catechist can easily modify the presentation during the second lesson to emphasize one or two of the points in the **Model Presentation.**

Following these two lesson plans is a page of suggestions for further lessons (**Mini-Lesson Plans**) on this topic. These lesson suggestions can be used to supplement the two primary plans when students manifest a desire for further study and reflection on the topic of the lesson. In such cases, these "mini-lessons" provide the kernel or core for five distinct lessons. These will be especially helpful for Catholic school classes which meet more than three times per week.

Some lessons also contain a **Catechist Resource Sheet.** This resource sheet contains additional ideas and quotations which will enrich the catechist's understanding of the material covered in the lesson plans.

In addition to the nine lessons, this book contains several other helpful features. The tenth lesson is a review methodology which teachers have found helpful in bringing together the many ideas covered in this unit. A special weekend retreat based on the Old Testament is also included. It adds a dimension of experiential learning to an otherwise academic program and is especially valuable for those who view youth ministry as something wider than formal academic training.

Each volume of the *Mine Is The Morning* series comes with a packet of duplicator masters. The purpose of these masters is to provide each group of students (usually about three to a group) with a copy of the task or study sheets. An examination of the lesson plans will reveal how this sheet is at the core of the learning experience.

Ideas for Special People

from the authors

For the Catholic school teacher

No one knows how difficult it is to sustain interest in religious studies in a Catholic school except those who have tried to teach religion. The charismatically gifted instructor may hold groups of teenagers spellbound class after class, year after year. The problem is that most of us who have taught or are teaching in Catholic schools are not charismatically gifted. We are believing people with some knowledge of theology and a love of youth. We do our best, even when that best seems meager indeed.

Mine Is the Morning can help you in your role as a teacher of religion in a Catholic school. Each lesson contains two fully extended lesson plans, pages of background material and at least five suggestions for further development of the topics presented in each lesson.

Classes which meet three times per week will find that one lesson per week is a good pace. On the first two days of the week we suggest the use of the primary and alternate lesson plans. On the third day, change the routine by using one of the mini-lesson plans. The variety here will bring new life to the class and make this third day special.

If your class meets more than three times per week, you may cover more lessons—possibly two per week. There are over 90 lessons in the series and consequently no shortage of material. At times it will be good to break the routine of class work and undertake one of the projects suggested under the title **Experiential Living and Learning** toward the end of the book. They will bring new life and vigor to the course.

For the novice CCD teacher

If you are a little uneasy entering a high school CCD program, know that all of us who have gone before you were nervous, too. In *Mine Is the Morning* you will find the kind of help that makes it difficult to go wrong. Before every lesson is a section entitled, **Catechist's Background.** This will give you the confidence you need. The Model Presentation will be your guide when you speak to the students and the lesson plans are completely worked out. Nothing is left to chance.

There is more richness in the lessons than you will ever use in class. Most CCD programs use the primary lesson plans only. These are the easiest to teach. Begin with them and as your confidence grows add some of the alternate lesson plans. When you are feeling fully confident look at the mini-lesson plans and take a stab at one or two of them. You may be surprised how easy it is to be a leader in the field of experiential catechesis.

Be of good heart. You can be a successful catechist. Pray often and ponder what you are learning. As you grow in your own capacity to understand Jesus and his Church you will become an increasingly valuable resource person to the youth you teach. Only time can bring all this about.

For the experienced CCD teacher

You know that no course, no new book, is going to change the face of the teenage world. Correct? Well, as authors of this series, we agree. The problems inherent in the catechesis of youth are largely cultural and faith-centered. Pedagogy can go only so far in solving those problems. Yet, why not have the best pedagogy possible and so save yourself agony and your students unnecessary boredom?

Mine Is the Morning contains, we think, the best pedagogy and theology available anywhere. It is experience-centered and yet not formless rap after rap after rap. The program is structured and is theologically sound. You will find in the **Catechist's Background** essays, the **Model Presentations,** the **Pondering Points** and the **Catechist's Resource Sheets** a wealth of information. You will also discover a variety of prayer experiences and some excellent, practical lesson plans.

What more can you ask of a high school series?

For those in youth ministry

Youth ministry is important. The new awareness of the need youth have for services in addition to the strictly catechetical will help the Church in the next decade. We think so highly of youth ministry that we explained our ideas in a book, *Parish Youth Ministry: A Manual for Beginners in the Art* (Twenty-Third Publications, P. O. Box 180, West Mystic, CT 06388).

But like all new movements, youth ministry has a tendency to forget its origins, the catechetical mission of the parish. We hope you will not become so enamored of social service, community building and liturgy that you allow your program to undersell regular religious education, even if you can offer it to only a minority of your flock. Studies show that this kind of instruction counts in forming attitudes of religiosity in youth. We neglect such programs only at the price of having to rebuild them later.

Thoughts About Teenagers

No one has yet captured the *zeitgeist* (that is the over-all situation) of teen-land in a few paragraphs, no more than anyone has yet captured adulthood in the same manner. Teens are people, all sorts of people, balanced and unbalanced, mature and immature, bright and not so bright, happy and melancholy. There is nothing unusual about all this for it is true of any group of people. In the classroom, each child is different and his differences, to one degree or another, determine what happens in the class. You must prepare well for a class, and be ready to move in another direction whenever the needs of the individual demand it. This will occur more often than you may suspect.

With this said, there are some characteristics which are more common in teen years than in adult or childhood years. One of these is a sense of boredom. The wild discovery of childhood has given way to the slower tempo of adolescence. The patience of adulthood has not yet been attained. This leaves the youth with neither sustaining feature and thus he is easily bored. For the teacher, this means the need to keep classes moving at a fairly rapid pace or the class will give in to natural boredom, and thus lose all interest.

The adolescent is just coming to grips with the sanctity of his own personality and is not at all sure of it. By turns he is dependent and independent. The teacher finds this difficult. How does one present the message of Jesus with authority, and yet preserve respect for the independence of the youth? This can best be done by steering away from rules and concentrating on the message itself, being more concerned with attitudes than with behavior. It can also be of help to say, "This is what I believe and have found helpful. You may come to a different conclusion but I hope you will consider my beliefs as you form your own."

The teenager is affected by heroes. Jesus is such a hero and can and should have a profound effect on youth. We can achieve this best by letting Jesus speak for himself, out of the New Testament. Church rules and other adult statements, while important, cannot have the effect of the words of Jesus himself.

Being children of their time, today's youth have a profound suspicion of organized anything. It is difficult to represent any organized institution. The Church is no exception. Realizing this, the careful teacher will not neglect the ecclesiastical dimension of his/her religion, but will emphasize the personal, Jesus-centered aspect whenever possible.

Youngsters will shock adults, if adults are willing to be shocked. A staid, unflappableness is essential for the good teacher.

Youth are easily turned to melancholy. Much of their music tells us this. Melancholy is not a gift of the Holy Spirit. Neither is guilt. The attitude of the teacher should not reinforce either of these emotions. The more the teacher can communicate the feeling of acceptance and of self-esteem the more the youth will prosper.

In a word, what the adolescent needs is a friendly, believing adult who cares about him. This attitude is more important than any amount of knowledge of content or technique.

Catechists who have been actively teaching for more than a few years recognize that every group of students has a character of its own. Some groups are able to verbalize their feelings well, some are not. Some groups are blessed with at least a few intelligent youngsters who initiate and carry on good conversation, other groups are almost mute. Some groups, for whatever mixture of chemistry of personality are always a discipline problem, others are so docile you wish for some disruption. Some groups relate well together, and with a catechist, others cannot get along together, or fail to relate to the catechist. Before you get discouraged and feel you are a failure, look into the history of the group with other catechists from past years. If several describe them as you find them, then just put your chin up and go right on. If, on the other hand, they were happy with a past catechist and seem unresponsive with you, learn the secret of the other catechist.

The catechist's role is not to be the person with all the answers which are imparted to the attentive ears of waiting students. S/he is one who leads the whole group (self included) into the world of discovery. S/he may not know a great deal more than the students, but can command their respect if like them, s/he is serious in the pursuit of knowledge and grace. To be one who commands respect, the catechist needs to be prepared, and so, in the words of the boy scout motto, BE PREPARED!

Our Theological Position

Teachers and students alike may wonder why we study the Old Testament when we ourselves are members of the new covenant. Students may question the wisdom of spending valuable time pondering the problems of people who lived centuries before Jesus himself.

The answer is a simple one. No one can understand Jesus without understanding the culture in which he worked and spoke his message. A knowledge of the Old Testament is a knowledge of Jesus' culture and his way of life. Moreover, the Old Testament accounts provide us with an unparalleled record of humanity's relationship with God. Humanity has not changed since those times nor, of course, has God. The lessons of the bible have timeless value.

Father Raymond Brown, the noted biblical scholar, has suggested that those who wish to understand what it is to live out a religious conviction over the long haul should look not to the New Testament but to the Old.

To understand what it is to live out our Christian conviction, then, we must turn to the Jewish scriptures, that exciting record of some twelve hundred years of the ups and downs of personal and institutional faith. We must search there for some keys to understanding who and what we Christians are and how we must behave. Not to know our history is to be condemned to repeat it.

And that may be the most interesting point to anyone who studies the Jewish scriptures—how often we Christians have already repeated the experiences of our early Jewish forebears. The history of the Christian church is filled with parallels to the lives lived by the Jewish people, to their desire for security and power, to their temporary reforms, to their regular reawakening to the mission God gave them. Everywhere one looks in the pages of the Old Testament he or she finds the prototype for Christian history and for contemporary life as well.

In our treatment of these fascinating books we have tried to concentrate on the meanings of the stories rather than on historical detail, although the details themselves would provide an interesting high school religion course for bright and well motivated students. Our choice of treating the stories in light of their meaning and application to our lives is based on the belief that most students in high school religion classes are intensely involved in their own developing world and have a less than avid interest in history.

The chart which follows illustrates how the material has been organized around the general theme of living out a religious conviction within a religious institution.

Event	Meaning
Lesson 1 Abraham's call and sacrifice of Isaac	Personal faith is always the root of all religious experience. Such faith requires sacrifice.
Lesson 2 The exodus	Personal faith leads to liberation.
Lesson 3 Covenant in the desert	Freedom and faith lead to the need for community.
Lesson 4 Receiving the law	Living in community leads to a need for law.
Lesson 5 Judges and Samuel	In the Jewish experience some good men always opposed the concentration of power.
Lesson 6 David as king	In the Jewish experience some good men always desired and worked for the concentration of power.
Lesson 7 David and his son Absalom	A dedication to an ideal usually brings with it isolation and misunderstanding.
Lesson 8 Elijah and the pre-exilic prophets	The prophets constantly called Israel to renew its faith.
Lesson 9 Isaiah (deutero) and early Genesis	The late prophets and the wisdom writers were early theologians who gave Israel a meaning system.

Content Analysis

Lesson	Catechist's Background	Model Presentation	Pondering Point	Catechist Resource Sheet
1	An explanation of the sources of the Book of Genesis and the idea of faith in the bible.	Abraham, the man of faith	Abraham and modern mobility	A timeline of the Old and New Testaments
2	A presentation of the personality traits of Moses revealed in Exodus; an explanation of freedom in biblical literature.	Moses led his people to freedom—a consequence of faith.	Black Americans and freedom	
3	An explanation of covenant and community in Exodus and in the New Testament.	Moses built the Israelite community.	Religious life and community	The books of the bible
4	An explanation of the formation of law in general and Israelite law in particular.	Moses protected freedom and community with law.	Law and freedom	Selections from canon law
5	An explanation of the historical background and the theology of the Book of Judges.	The Judges were a voice calling Israel to its covenant commitment.	The American Labor Movement	
6	An explanation of the history of David's rise to power, his unification of Israel and his symbolic significance to later generations.	David unified the community.	The role of bishops	A map of David's kingdom
7	An explanation of the latter years of David's reign.	David did not find complete fulfillment in his community of faith.	Isolation within community	The principal characters of the David story
8	An explanation of the history of the divided kingdom and the influence of the prophets.	Elijah and the subsequent prophets call Israel to its own ideas.	Our century's prophet	The idea of prophet and some of the great prophets
9	An explanation of the relationship of faith and knowledge and the role of theology in Israel.	Deutero-Isaiah, parts of Genesis, Job, Jonah and other Old Testament books are reflective theology at its best.	John Courtney Murray	The Catholic theological story

Special Suggestions for this volume

The following suggestions should help the catechist enrich the classroom material:

1. Prepare ahead. Some advance planning is absolutely necessary for the alternative lesson plans. A chart follows this section. This chart will identify the areas of special preparation and thus allow the catechist to decide early which alternative lessons are practical in his or her circumstances.
2. Prepare for the Recap (Lesson 10). This can be done by keeping a record of all student work on newsprint or butcher paper during each class, storing these and bringing them out for the recap lesson. These will also provide the teacher with a clear record of the class if it is to be taught a second time. Failing this public record, the teacher should have one of the students keep a class notebook in which all the reporting is recorded.
3. Music can enrich the class. The spirituals of Black America are ideal for this purpose when studying the Old Testament since they capture much of the futuristic longing common to Jewish history.
4. This volume contains a wide selection of Old Testament prayers. These may be read slowly to the students or easily duplicated and read in a group. If the catechist wants to make the most of these prayers we suggest that he or she take the time to prepare a short introduction to them, add some background music, and provide the time necessary for meditation after reading them.
5. A few good but simple references on the bible are necessary. Following are some examples:
    a. *The Jerusalem Bible,* or another standard edition, has excellent introductions to each of the Bible books.
    b. *The Dictionary of the Bible* by John L. McKenzie, originally published by Bruce Publishing Company, Milwaukee in 1965, is perhaps the best, easy-to-use source of biblical information for the teacher.
    c. The American Bible Society, 1865 Broadway, New York, NY 10023, has an inexpensive booklet containing the psalms. Where budgets permit, students could well profit from receiving a copy of these prayers of the Old Testament and the early church.
    d. One final tool that is recommended is a concordance, available in all libraries. The concordance contains a list of all words used in the Bible. This allows a student to look up almost any subject with ease.

This unit can be completed in as few as nine meetings or expanded to 18 by using the primary and alternate lesson plans or even beyond 18 by using the suggested mini-lesson plans. To make use of the wealth of activities in this unit the catechist must plan ahead.

The following **checklist** is to help you do just that.

___1. Read all the catechist's background essays, model presentations and lesson plans.
___2. Check the **Materials Needed** section of each lesson plan to be certain they are available or can be ordered in time.
___3. Make sure you have access to a spirit duplicator machine for running off copies of the spirit masters provided with this program.
___4. Check your diocesan religious education office catalogue for available records, films, filmstrips, and other aids which can enrich your presentation.
___5. Do not hesitate to order catalogues from various religious education publishers.
___6. If a visit to a community is to be used (Lesson 3, alternate plan), arrangements should be made at least three weeks in advance. See page 58.
___7. If a study of *The Lord of the Flies* is to be used (Lesson 4, alternate plan), three copies of the book should be borrowed from the library or purchased from a book store. This book is available in paperback.
___8. If a filmstrip is to be used in Lesson 5, alternate plan, order it several weeks in advance from your diocesan filmstrip library or the publisher. See page 90.
___9. If the class is to meet with the parish council (Lesson 6, alternate plan), arrangements should be made several weeks in advance of the proposed meeting.
___10. If a guest speaker will speak to the students (Lesson 9, alternate plan), he or she should be invited at least three weeks in advance. See page 150.
___11. If you plan to use any of the Mini Lesson Plans at the end of each lesson, the materials needed should be ordered well in advance. The list of materials needed is too long to be given here.
___12. If you plan An Old Testament Weekend (Experiential Living and Learning), make all arrangements well in advance. Read thoroughly the descriptive material on page 158.

Planning Chart

Topic	Goal	Methodologies	

Lesson 1

Abraham: Finding a God to Believe In | To show how faith brings with it the necessity of sacrifice. | 1. Study of impact of a new relationship on existing ones.
2. Analysis of the similarity between friendship and faith. | 3. Mini plans
  a. Time line study
  b. The faith experience
  c. Filmstrip study— Abraham
  d. Read and report
  e. Geneological table

Lesson 2

Free At Last | To show how every believer is called to freedom. | 1. Ranking contemporary forms of slavery in order of destructiveness.
2. Comparison study— American slavery, ghetto life, slavery of Hebrews. | 3. Mini plans
  a. Cardinal Mindszenty
  b. Caesar Chavez
  c. Life in the ghetto
  d. The Campaign for Human Development

Lesson 3

Forming a People | To show how all believers need community. | 1. Study of glue that holds communities together.
2. Visit to a group living in community. | 3. Mini plans
  a. The Jewish bible
  b. A film
  c. A filmstrip
  d. The Amish
  e. Community development

Lesson 4

The Lawgiver | To show how all who live in community need a law. | 1. Forming a code of conduct for marooned teenagers.
2. Study of *Lord of the Flies*. | 3. Mini plans
  a. Canon Law
  b. Filmstrip study
  c. Invite a Rabbi
  d. A good discussion

Lesson 5

The Voice of Discontent | To show that living in community demands a critical stance. | 1. Analyzing criticism's effect on community.
2. Filmstrip on Samuel | 3. Mini plans
  a. Cathedral films
  b. Cowboy stories
  c. Role play
  d. Map making
  e. Newspapers

Lesson 6

| The Voice of Practicality | To show that living in community demands a cooperative stance. | 1. Analysis— youth needs in the parish
2. Dialogue with parish council members | 3. Mini plans
   a. Bible research
   b. David the conquerer
   c. Filmstrip study
   d. David and Goliath
   e. David the valiant |

Lesson 7

| The Price of Faith | To show how faith usually brings with it some isolation. | 1. Writing a story ending.
2. Role play— courtroom scene | 3. Mini plans
   a. Relationships with others
   b. The Psalms
   c. Absalom or David
   d. David as model of Jesus
   e. Solomon's temple |

Lesson 8

| Prophecy | To show how we should react to our prophets. | 1. Identifying prophets in our contemporary world.
2. Research gospels for allusions to the prophets. | 3. Mini plans
   a. Indian viewpoints
   b. Martin Luther King, Jr.
   c. Role Playing
   d. Imagine a prophet
   e. Research prophets |

Lesson 9

| New Theologies | To show how we should react to our theologians. | 1. Comparison study— traditional and folk hymns
2. Speaker— changes since Vatican II | 3. Mini plans
   a. The book of Isaiah
   b. Theologians
   c. Invitation
   d. Filmstrip studies in theology |

Lesson 10

| Recap | To help the students review and evaluate the topics covered and the discussions held during this unit. | 1. Unit review |

Experiential Living and Learning

| An Old Testament Weekend | To prepare and participate in a weekend retreat based on the Old Testament. |

1 Abraham: Finding a God to Believe In

CATECHIST'S BACKGROUND

The Book of Genesis

The word *genesis* means origins or beginnings. In the Book of Genesis the reader finds a wide-brush picture of human history from the beginning of creation until the time of the Israelite departure from Egypt. The stories are told by master theologians who chose and assembled their material to illustrate their point: *God loves His special people and is directing them toward some as yet mysterious goal.*

Bible scholars are not completely certain how this first book of the bible came to be written in its present form. They guess that oral traditions, family history, ballads and cultic prayers existed from the time of Abraham (about 1750 B.C.). Probably a group of religious leaders in the Southern Kingdom sometime in the 10th century B.C. were the first to weave these many stories into a single narrative. This narrative is characterized by profound psychological insights, excellent descriptions of people and places, and the use of the word *Yahweh* for God.

A second group of religious leaders in the Northern Kingdom, probably after the reform of the prophet Isaiah (sometime after 850 B.C.), compiled a second narrative in which they refused to use the name Yahweh for events before the desert covenant and instead used *Elohim*. This narrative lacks some of the color and insight of the earlier collection.

Much later after the Babylonian exile (perhaps 539 B.C.), the priests of Jerusalem added a collection of stories and laws of their own. This collection is often redundant and very legalistic.

A fourth collection of stories and laws, the Deuteronomic, is found only rarely in Genesis. It is limited for the most part to the fifth book of the Old Testament, Deuteronomy.

This brief overview gives some idea of the complexity of the material with which the teacher must deal when treating the Book of Genesis. The original stories go back to a period almost 2,000 years before Christ. They were preserved as folklore for 1,000 years before being written in the first of the narrative forms. Narrations were put together over a period of 500 years and only given a final editing sometime after the exile in Babylon.

Because the Hebrew people had a high regard for tradition, however, they did preserve their own origins with amazing accuracy. Contemporary historical study has shown how the lives of the patriarchs as recorded in *Genesis* conform exactly to the lives people at that period led. Even when later bible writers did not understand their material they were loath to change it. A careful reading of the Abraham stories, for example, will reveal contradictions which are difficult, if not impossible, to unravel. These contradictions must have been apparent to editors and compilers of earlier times. They could have rewritten the stories but did not. They chose, instead, to keep alive the traditions rather than pass any judgement on their historical accuracy.

Abraham

Abraham lived about 1750 B.C.. With his family he migrated from the desert area east of Palestine into the Tigris and

Euphrates valleys. Such migrations were common at the time. Later, again with his family, he migrated to what is now Northern Palestine. Leaving his family he passed into Palestine proper and there lived out his life. One series of stories also takes him to Egypt and back to Palestine.

The authors of *Genesis* indicate that Abraham was the first to believe in the one God. He is presented as a person of faith, one driven onward by a divine compulsion and a promise that his descendants would be a great nation. Many of the stories told of him seem to be barbaric and even contrived but each serves the authors' purpose, to show how God loved His people and established them as a special nation.

The idea of faith

Abraham is, according to Saint Paul, the model of faith. He is a person whose life is founded on faith in the Lord, a person whose every act is in response to his personal relationship with this mysterious God.

Paul notes that, before any peoplehood or legal tradition had been established, Abraham had faith. For Paul, faith is prior to and more important than any religious act or any lineage. This faith is a personal act made in response to an invitation from the Lord. This reliance upon faith is reborn, again according to Paul, in the Christian era when faith in the Lord Jesus becomes the foundation of a new people and the basic ingredient of a new moral life.

Catholics of our generation have begun to place more and more emphasis on the act of personal faith. During the immigrant years of the Church in North America, belonging to the Church was the prime goal of religious leaders. Faced with masses of unlettered immigrants living in a hostile culture, leaders found it necessary to insist on behavioral conformity to Church laws and the importance of membership within the Church. Without this underpinning, these leaders felt that personal faith would have no sound foundation on which to build. Unfortunately, many Catholics of this age came to think that membership and conformity to Church law were all that were necessary for the religious life.

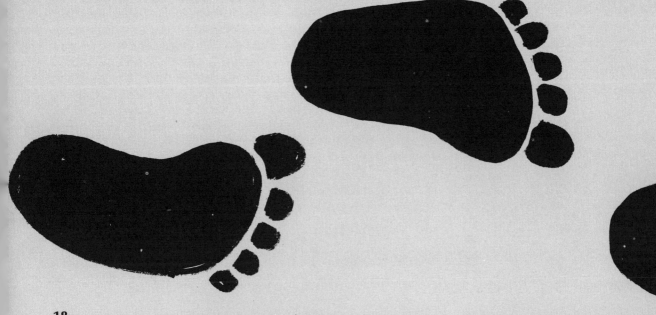

Since Vatican II Catholics have been busy correcting this misinterpretation. Modern religious education, the Charismatic movement, the retreat movement, the Marriage Encounter movement, and a host of other reforms have reestablished the importance of personal faith in the lives of Catholics.

In this lesson we have highlighted two characteristics of personal faith: loneliness and sacrifice. The best Catholic tradition has spoken of the progress in the spiritual life as a lonely one, one marked by misunderstanding and the struggle to discover God within one's innermost self. Saint Teresa of Avila, Saint John of the Cross and Saint Ignatius of Loyola are all excellent witnesses of this tradition.

A personal faith also requires sacrifice. In the words of modern Values Clarification theory, the person of faith establishes a priority among his or her values. At the top of this list is a relationship with the Lord. The maintenance of this relationship means that other legitimate pleasures in life must often be set aside in order to keep this prime relationship intact. In older terminology, this "setting aside" was called sacrifice. Actually, the word sacrifice in its root meaning means just this.

Pedagogy

The **Primary Lesson Plan** asks students to comment on what happens to a young person who has fallen in love. This is then used as a model for understanding faith. The **Model Presentation** discusses Abraham as a person of deep personal faith. The **Alternate Lesson Plan** requires students to make symbols of friendship and to discuss its meaning. This discussion then leads into a discussion of faith as a personal friendship with the Lord.

The **Mini Lesson Plans** suggest a study of an Old Testament time line, an interview with a Charismatic Catholic, a filmstrip study, a report on Ignatius of Loyola's famous meditation, The Two Standards, and the experience of making a geneological table.

The **Catechist Resource Sheet** contains a time line beginning at 1800 B.C. and ending with the present day.

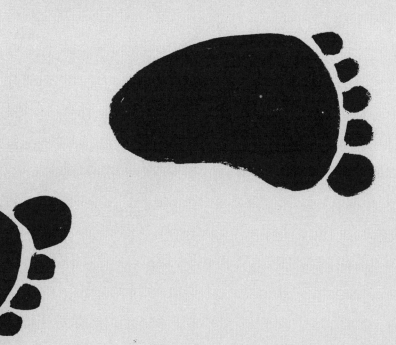

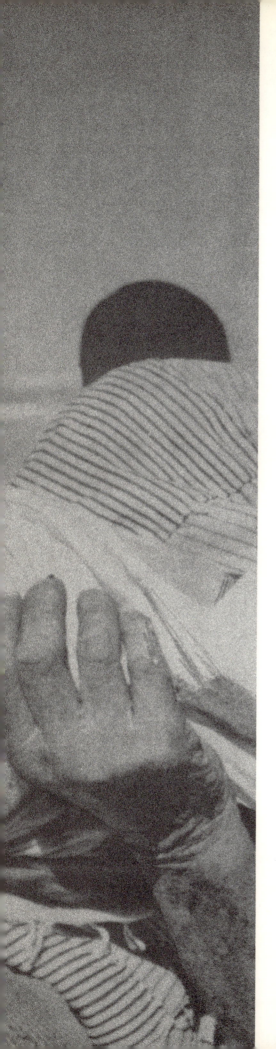

MODEL PRESENTATION
"Finding a God to Believe In"

Topics to be presented:

1. Abraham followed wherever God led him.
2. Abraham was willing to sacrifice his most precious possession in order to retain his friendship with God.
3. Faith today requires of us this same willingness to sacrifice and to follow.

Abraham the follower

Abraham was an ordinary young man, a man of his time and culture. His father, Terah, was a desert nomad whose relentless search for better pasture for his flocks and water for his family had taken him out of the desert to the town of Ur. From Ur he led his family into what is now Northern Palestine. In all these wanderings Abraham, or Abram as he was then called, followed his father's lead.

Then, in some mysterious way, God called Abraham apart from his family. Always obedient to the Lord, Abraham embarked upon an extraordinary adventure. Again and again, the Lord called upon him to seek new lands and new directions. In the midst of his wanderings the Lord gave Abram the new name of Abraham, the name by which we know him. God also made a covenant with his friend and promised that he would become the father of many nations. So numerous would his descendants become, the Lord promised, that they would be like the grains of sand on the seashore or the stars in the skies.

Throughout his life Abraham was always on the move, always following the messages of the Lord which sounded in his heart. Even though he knew little of this God, Abraham never hesitated to follow wherever He led.

Abraham's sacrifice

Like all men of his day Abraham wanted sons, his own sons. Young men who would carry his name and celebrate his exploits in their songs and campfire stories. Living on through his children's memories was the only kind of immortality Abraham ever dreamed about.

Yet, this desire for his own son was the one thing God seemed unwilling to give him. Abraham's flocks prospered. His enemies fell before his mighty sword. His slaves respected him. Yet, he had no son of his own. He did have children by slave wives, children who might inherit his wealth, wax rich and even powerful but somehow slave children were not the same. The laws of the day permitted Abraham as many wives as he could support but it was a child by his first wife, Sarah, which alone would bring him contentment. This would be his full-fledged child and heir.

Then mysteriously when Abraham was in advanced old age and Sarah herself was long past the age for childbearing, Abraham received his longed-for son. If ever a child was the apple of his father's eye, it was young Isaac. Abraham saw in Isaac his whole future, the fulfillment of all his dreams of becoming a great nation as God had promised him.

Young Isaac showed promise of becoming all that Abraham dreamed he might become. Then, just as Isaac was entering adolescence, the mysterious God Abraham worshipped asked of him the impossible sacrifice. The Lord commanded Abraham to immolate his son, to kill and burn his body on the altar. This idea of human sacrifice was not strange or violent in Abraham's age. It was a part of daily life, a taken-for-granted reality. Such offering to the gods was common enough. But to offer this son, this only son, this son of his old age was the supreme test of faith.

How many restless nights Abraham spent pondering his response to God are not recorded in the bible story. All that is recorded is his resolve to obey as simply and as resolutely as his old body would allow. With his beloved son, Isaac, Abraham journeyed to the mountain. There he unsheathed his knife and began the ritual of sacrifice.

God was pleased by Abraham's faith. He stayed Abraham's hand, snatched Isaac from the jaws of death and restored him to his father. What mattered on that mountain top was not so much the salvation of Isaac from death so much as the resolute and unflinching faith of his father, Abraham.

The meaning of faith

To this day, the word faith among Jews, Mohammedans and Christians recalls Abraham. Abraham is still the model of faith, the man whose life tells us what it means to be a believer.

Abraham's faith called him apart. It called him away from his family and even demanded of him the sacrifice of his only son. Faith today is much the same. It is not merely saying we believe in some special words others have placed in our mouths. No, it is so much more!

Faith is a personal response to God speaking in us. When we follow God, we discover that we are moving apart from others into a kind of loneliness. No one else understands what is happening within us as we respond to God's call. Our faith leads us to pilgrimage and this pilgrimage leads, in turn, to long lonely moments when only God can understand.

This faith often demands sacrifice. It means more than giving up something we know is harmful to us or evil. Faith can demand that we leave behind things which seem good and even necessary in order to follow the Lord. No two people are called upon to leave behind the same thing at the same time but all are called upon to sacrifice.

Teens today, all of you, are much like Abraham in the desert. You must wander in search of something not yet certain. Some of this wandering will be done with others, family friends and school mates, but the final trip to the mountain of sacrifice will be yours alone. Only then will you have a faith tried by sacrifice, a faith completely your own.

To be a person of faith, then, is more than belonging to the right group or even doing the correct things. Faith is placing yourself at the disposal of God, following where He leads, giving Him whatever He asks. Such faith is the faith we celebrate each time we remember Abraham, that man who lived so long ago.

PONDERING POINT

Abraham and Mobility

Most North American families have much in common with Abraham and the other patriarchs. That common bond is recent immigration from Europe and perhaps one or more family relocations since that experience. Like Abraham, many moderns are semi-nomads.

The experience of relocation can either build or destroy one's religious commitment. Some of the Europeans who migrated to North America, especially those who settled in areas with few Church services, easily lost their religious traditions. Others, probably the vast majority, developed a deeper commitment and a more intense loyalty to their Church because of the immigration. Living in a new land stripped of many of the cultural supports for religion, a great number of immigrant Americans took religion seriously and personalized their inherited traditions. For this reason, the Catholic Church in North America has been able to claim a deeply felt allegiance among great numbers of people whereas European Churches often number only a small active minority of their respective populations.

Migration to new cities and states, to new provinces and different subcultures within North America has had a similar effect on religious practice. Some people used their moving as an escape from religion. Others found in the continued practice of it an important continuity with their past and an easy step to acceptance within their new locale.

Migration of people works two ways, then. It both intensifies and deadens religious practice. In the case of Abraham, migration continually intensified his religious feeling and brought him to new heights of divine awareness.

PRIMARY LESSON PLAN

CLASS PLAN

Goal:
To show how faith brings with it the necessity of sacrifice.

Materials needed:
1) Copies, one per group of three, of the Task Sheet provided with this program. See page 29.
2) Blank paper, pencil for each student
3) Blackboard, chalk and eraser
4) Newsprint, marking pen, masking tape

Methodology:
1. Using the Task Sheet, the students will study the impact of a new relationship on existing relations in the life of an imaginary teenager.
2. The catechist, using the material from the Model Presentation, "Finding a God to Believe In," will tell the story of Abraham and show how his new faith relationship with God made changes in his other relationships a necessity. This change in other relationships is what we often call sacrifice.

Opening prayer:
God, our Father,
You called Abraham out of the desert
    and into the land of promise.
As he pilgrimaged he learned to believe.
You have called me, too, out of my deserts
    of self-doubt and confusion
Into the promised land of your kingdom,
    a place of confidence and peace.
As I make my pilgrimage,
    may I, too, learn to believe in you
    with my heart as well as with my head.
Amen.

Opening remarks:
Today we begin a study of the people of the bible before the time of Christ and the Gospels. This part of the bible is composed largely of books about incomparable heroes, great men and women who, for all their greatness, are very much like the rest of us. As we trace the course of history through Abraham to Jesus we will be looking for more than mere historical knowledge. We will be trying to learn what happens to people who, like us, are born into a faith and then try to live it the way God commands.

Task Sheet *Allow about 15 minutes.*

Today we will be talking about the impact of a new relationship on our old relationships. To do this, I would like you to break into groups of three students each and look at the Task Sheet we will be working with. *(Give out sheet and pencils to each group.)* It tells the story of John, an imaginary high-schooler, who falls in love. You are asked to discuss what effect his new lovelife will have on other people in his life. Take about fifteen minutes to get your answers together and then we will share them.

Reporting:

(Use newsprint to save for the recap or the blackboard.)

Now, let's look at No. 1 on our Task Sheet. I'll list all of your ideas on newsprint. *(Call on each group, allow time for comments from other groups.)* Good, now let's look at No. 2. *(Repeat the process for each of the questions.)*

Discussion:

(Lead the students into a more abstract understanding with questions like the following:)

a) What impact is John's new relationship having on his older ones? Why must this be so?
b) Can you think of other examples of a new relationship changing older ones?
c) Have you ever thought of faith as a new relationship? Why is faith a relationship? Why can we call it a new relationship even though people are baptized as infants?

SAVE POSTERS for the recap, Lesson 10. See Special suggestion No. 2, page 11.

Bridging:

Now that we have talked about new relationships and especially about that new relationship of faith, let me share with you the story of the first man we know of who believed in the true God. His name was Abraham. Before we begin, take a sheet of paper and write: "If I were a member of Abraham's family I would have wondered about . . ." We will discuss your answers after my short presentation.

Presentation:
Use the material from the Model Presentation, "Finding a God to Believe In."

Discussion:

a) Who will volunteer his or her answer? What do the rest of you think of this answer? Is it realistic? Why? Why not? *(Call on other volunteers for answers.)*
b) What effect did Abraham's believing have on his life?
c) Do you know others who began to take their faith seriously and have had to make sacrifices?
d) Do you think you have made any sacrifices for your faith? Explain. *(The catechist may wish to share some personal experiences at this point.)*

Closing prayer:

Lord, you said to Abraham:
I will bless those who bless you,
I will curse those who slight you.
All the tribes of the earth
    will bless themselves by you.
You so loved Abraham. He was your special friend.
May I, too, share in that friendship
    which we call faith.
And, may I be willing to make the sacrifices
    believing always brings. Amen, Lord. Amen.

Bible References

The whole of Genesis 12-25 is a collection of the stories of Abraham. Passages you might especially enjoy are:

Abraham's Call	12:1-9
Melchizedek	14:17-24
God's Promise	15:1-21
Sacrifice of Isaac	22:1-19

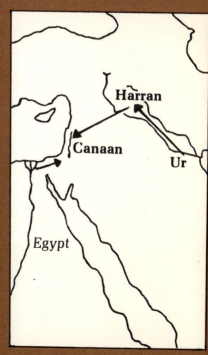

ABRAHAM'S ROUTE FROM UR TO CANAAN

ALTERNATE PLAN

CLASS PLAN

Goal:

To show how faith brings with it the necessity of sacrifice.

Materials needed:

1) Large assortment of creative art materials including construction paper, marking pens, pencils, paper, scissors, glue, tape
2) Picture magazines, newspapers
3) Large tables to work on or area to spread out
4) Newsprint, marking pen, masking tape
5) Bible

Methodology:

1. The students will make symbols which express the experience of friendship. They will then explain the meaning of the symbols to the class.

2. The catechist will lead a discussion of the similarity between friendship and faith and note the similarity between the symbols used to express both concepts.

3. The catechist will present or review the material from the Model Presentation, "Finding a God to Believe In," and show how Abraham was led into a deep personal friendship with the Lord.

Opening prayer:

Lord, God, mighty in your creative act,
    gentle in your reaching out to Israel,
    king in your daily care for the world's little ones,
Grant me the gift of loving faith.
Let me be your friend,
    —Awake and aware of your presence in my life,
    —Filled with concern for you and yours,
    —Ready to spend my days in your exciting company.
Give me that friendship people here call faith.
Amen.

Opening comments:

One experience most of us have had is friendship. This experience is one of the most important ones in our lives. Usually friendships begin when we are about ten years old, although there are those who have close friends before that. In early adolescence we enlarge our experience of friendship to include members of the other sex. Ultimately, most of us will find one person of the other sex and cherish him or her as our closest, life-long friend in marriage.

Closely akin to the friendships we have with human beings is our friendship with God—what theologians call faith. But, more about faith later. For the present, we will try to think about and express the experience of being a friend.

Project:

What I would like you to do for the next half hour is to use any of the materials I have assembled to express in your own way what it means to be a friend. You may write a poem, make a collage, draw a picture, compose a symbol—do anything you like that will convey to others your feelings about friendship. You may work alone or in groups of two or three.

Does everyone understand what we are doing? Any questions? You can begin now and when you are finished I will ask you to show your work and let the class respond to it. *(Be prepared to answer their questions.)*

Allow 30 minutes for the project.

Reporting/Discussion:

Now, let's ask each person or group to show us what they have done.

(As the first object is presented, ask some of the following questions of the class and of the presenter. Repeat this process for all presentations.)

1. What kind of a feeling do you get when you look at this object?
2. What thoughts does it suggest to you about friendship?
3. _____, are you communicating what you thought you would to the group? How so, how not? Are there other things you hoped your object would trigger in others which have not been mentioned? What are they?

(After the discussion, display the projects around the room.)

SAVE PROJECTS for the recap, Lesson 10. See Special Suggestion No. 2, page 11.

Catechist's presentation:

Here, the catechist may wish to review the Model Presentation, "Finding a God to Believe In," or, if the class has not done the primary lesson, present the material for the first time. An introduction to a first time presentation:

So far we have talked only about human relationships. Now let's talk about a friendship in which one person is God. We have an excellent record of such a friendship in the Book of Genesis. It is the story of Abraham, the earliest record we have of a believer in the true God.

Discussion:

a) Look around at the projects again. Do any of them symbolize well friendship with God? Which ones? Explain.
b) Do you think all friendships require sacrifice? Why?

Closing prayer:

Read or have a student read: John 15:12-17, Jesus says "You are my friends."

Friendship banners may be made from felt strips and bits of burlap.

Discuss 2 Chronicles 20:7 where God's friendship for Abraham is cited.

MINI LESSON PLANS

The purpose of the ideas which follow is to provide the creative teacher with further suggestions for classroom experiences related to the original Model Presentation.

Time Line Study

On page 30 is a time line showing the relative position of the Old Testament characters and events. This time line is not in the duplicator master packet but can be copied for each student. Students can each be given a character or event on the line, asked to research the assignment and then report to the whole class. This will provide a preliminary overview to the Old Testament before taking up detailed study. The introductory information before each bible book is usually adequate for this type of research.

The Faith Experience

Faith is at the root of the story of Abraham. A high school class can profit from an interview with a Charismatic Catholic since charismatics place great emphasis on the "baptism of the Holy Spirit," or in the terms of the traditional spiritual writers, the conversion experience. Such an interview will make the story of Abraham real in the students' eyes. As with all invitations to classroom visitors, the request should be made several weeks in advance and the students should be aware of the visit in time to formulate perceptive questions.

Filmstrip Study

Two filmstrips by Roa Films, 1696 North Astor Street, Milwaukee, WI 53202, *The Call of Abraham* and *The Sacrifice of Abraham* present the historical facts of the story in vivid sound and color. While these filmstrips are written for junior high, they can be used with the proper explanations. The teacher should provide the students with several questions they are to answer during the viewing. This technique will help them focus their attention.

Read and Report

Read and report to the class the famous meditation by Saint Ignatius Loyola on the two standards, the conversion experience. This, the most famous of all Christian meditations, is found in the first week of *The Spiritual Exercises*, a book which is available in most Catholic school or parish libraries. After hearing the report students might wish to spend time making the meditation together.

Geneological Table

Making a geneological table is a good way to understand the relationships between the early patriarchs of Israel. All the information necessary for such an exercise can be found in the Book of Genesis.

TASK SHEET 1

Falling in Love

John has been one of the outstanding students in your high school. He has maintained a B+ scholastic average, been captain of the track team and a good fullback for the school football squad. He is popular with his classmates and was recently elected to the student council. He spends a lot of time with some of his friends at the local hangout and gets along well with both his parents and brothers and sisters. He is an avid hiker and loves to go camping with a group of senior scouts.

This past week John met a girl who had just moved into town and entered his school. John thinks he is in love with this new girl, Betty, and wants to spend time with her on dates and just talking together at school and in the neighborhood.

What effect will John's new relationship with Betty have on:

1. His school work? _____

2. His athletics? _____

3. His work on the student council? _____

4. His friends? _____

5. His mother and father? _____

6. His brothers and sisters? _____

7. His interest in the senior scouts? _____

(Duplicator master of this sheet in packet)

CATECHIST RESOURCE SHEET

A TIMELINE OF THE OLD AND NEW TESTAMENT

- Abraham
- B.C. 1800

- Joseph
- 1600

- Micah
- Hosea
- Amos
- Elijah
- Isaiah

- Moses
- Exodus
- 1280-1240

- Judges

- Samuel Saul David Solomon
- 1040-1000   960

- Division into 2 kingdoms

- Fall of Northern Kingdom

- B.C. 922
- 721

- Babylonian Captivity
- Jeremiah Ezekiel
- 587-539

- Nehemiah
- Ezdra

- Rise of Maccabees
- 150

- Jesus
- Fathers of Church
- Constantine
- A.D. 33
- 400

- Height of Medieval times
- Dark Ages
- 800

- A.D. 1000

- Reformation
- 1600

- Vatican 1 Vatican 2
- 1900   1965

2
Free At Last

CATECHIST'S BACKGROUND

Moses

The same complex historical process which produced the *Book of Genesis* was at work in preserving the story of Moses and the Exodus. In fact, the first five books of the bible are a single unit. As in the case of Abraham, oral traditions preserved in family lore, cultic prayers, ballads and other forms of folk remembering were written down and edited over a 600 year period. The stories we have about Moses are undoubtedly accurate in their main outline. They are also, however, the product of heightened appreciation of his role by later generations, the inventions of pious Israelites who filled in the gaps in the oral traditions, and the work of legal scholars who wished to show that all Hebrew law enjoyed Moses' approval.

The picture of Moses given us in the many stories in this section of the Old Testament is, for all its variations, fairly consistent. Moses was a diffident, even hesitant person. He manifested an honest self-doubt about his ability to undertake the responsibilities of forming a people. This self-doubt is present in his flight from Egypt as a young man, his encounter with the Lord at the burning bush, his struggles with the Pharaoh, and even during his leadership in the desert. Such self-doubt and personal uncertainty can only endear him to modern people who know so much uncertainty in their own personal quest for faith.

A second characteristic of Moses was his brashness. He killed the Egyptian persecutor of his people, undertook to lead his own people and struggled with them against impossible odds. Such brashness is often associated with self-doubt in people even today. It seems that the diffident person breaks out of his hesitancy only by bold action.

The final characteristic of Moses which bears mention was his amazing perseverance. It was Moses who initiated the Hebrew struggle for freedom and he who never failed to direct his people toward their goal. This perseverance is remarkable in any person let alone one who must balance the whims and fancies of an entire people not yet formed by institutions and laws.

The Covenant

The highest achievement of Moses was the formation of a people who believed in the one God. This sense of a national relationship with the Lord was strong enough to survive the ages of the tribal confederation and the divided monarchy. It was present with the Jews in exile and strengthened their resolve to rebuild their holy city. This sense of God's impact upon Jewish life still remains among world Jewry after 2,000 years of homelessness. There are few if any parallels in human history to this achievement.

However Moses taught his people their special relationship with the Lord, he best proclaimed it with the Sinai covenant relationship. In this covenant, Yahweh, the God Moses revealed to his people, entered into a solemn agreement with the people of Israel. He agreed to be their God and they agreed to be His own people. Once this covenant was sealed

with public ceremonial, God remained faithful to it. Israel, however, had its ups and downs. At one time, Israel would be fervent in its special relationship. At another time, Israel would show unmistakable signs of weakness. Yet, in spite of this weakness, Israel under the prodding of the Lord and His prophets always returned to its covenant relationship.

The purpose of the Law in Israel was to show loyal believers how to maintain the covenant. There was to be no worship of alien gods, no mistreatment of fellow Hebrews, justice for the oppressed, and a scrupulous observance of religious tradition. As long as Israel was true to the Law, the covenant was intact. When Israel grew careless of the Law, the covenant relationship was violated. Yet, even in the beginning no formalism was permitted. True faithfulness meant more than mere external observance. Always underlying the covenant was some element of personal faith in the one God, however vaguely expressed.

Freedom

Because of the experience of Egyptian slavery and the later Babylonian exile, the Jewish nation prized its freedom in a way peculiar to a once-subjugated people. The meaning of the Exodus was a passage from slavery to freedom. The Hebrews were proud to announce that they were free people, people who owed allegiance only to the Lord.

The writers of the Old Testament did not expound abstractions about the nature and limits of human freedom. They did, however, celebrate the difference between living under the yoke and living as an independent nation. They did attempt to maximize the freedom of individuals by an intricate set of laws and customs which protected the weak from the powerful. They did proclaim the truth that before God all His people had worth and dignity.

For these ancient writers freedom was both a social condition and a personal possession. As a social condition, freedom came to Israel in the Exodus from Egypt. At various times it was lost because of their own carelessness with the Law but regained as they returned to the Law's practice. This social condition was not a matter of chance or of some blind forces of history. Rather, God gave them their freedom as a people, maintained that freedom for them, and took it from them only

to call them back to their covenant relationship. All political history was theological history. God supervised all the workings of kings and princes. He defeated or gave victory to armies to suit His own purpose.

Personal freedom belonged to each Israelite. Each person was able to obey the Law or disobey it. This Law commanded the rich to provide the minimum of protection and security for all members of the race in order that individuals might live in the dignity which belonged to the children of the Lord. This insistence upon the rights of the poor also safeguarded the individual's freedom to observe the covenant.

Freedom was, then, an important concept in both the national and personal lives of the Hebrew people. Much of our Christian preoccupation with freedom has its roots in the ancient traditions and beliefs of the Old Testament people.

Pedagogy

In this lesson we have chosen to highlight Moses as the liberator of his people. There are other aspects of Moses' remarkable career—his foundation of Israel, his concern for law and institution, his religious and cultic leadership. Yet, for the teenager the idea of faith leading to freedom seems most important.

The **Primary Lesson Plan** asks students to reflect on several kinds of slavery with which they are familiar at least through the media. The **Model Presentation** shows how Moses struggled to find personal freedom and then brought that freedom to others. This is then situated in our own Catholic tradition as the natural process of faith leading to freedom. The **Alternate Lesson Plan** takes a historical approach and asks the students to compare the slavery of the Hebrews in the Old Testament with the slavery of the black people in America.

The **Mini Lesson Plans** suggest a study of Cardinal Mindszenty and Caesar Chavez as modern examples of great leaders of people and liberators of the masses. Also suggested are a study of a modern account of ghetto slavery, and participation in the U.S. Bishops' Campaign for Human Development—one of today's most successful struggles against slavery in modern life.

MODEL PRESENTATION

"Free At Last"

Topics to be presented:

1. Because he was a man of faith, Moses brought freedom to his people.
2. History gives many examples of people who acted as Moses did.
3. Faith always leads toward freedom.

Moses

Moses is perhaps the most famous of all the Old Testament characters. It was he who brought freedom to Israel, who led the chosen people through the Red Sea and formed them into a nation in the desert wilderness. Almost everyone knows a little about Moses.

Born into slavery like his Hebrew brothers and sisters, Moses was saved from slavery's degradation by adoption into Pharaoh's own family. You no doubt remember the story of Moses in the basket, his discovery by Pharaoh's daughter and subsequent adoption. Now a lesser man than Moses would have enjoyed the luxury of his high estate and learned to despise the people from which he came.

But as a young adult, Moses returned to visit his people and saw them trapped in the most savage oppression. Enraged at the sight of the violence of an Egyptian toward a helpless Hebrew, Moses lashed out. In his blind fury he killed the Egyptian oppressor. With that, Moses' life was changed. From prince of the realm, Moses became a hunted man, an outlaw.

After years of hiding at the edge of the desert in Midian—years in which Moses again fashioned a comfortable existence—he was once more thrust into the fury of the conflict between his people and their oppressors. Moses met the Lord in the desert. From a burning bush the Lord commanded him to return to his brothers and sisters in Egypt and set them free. Moses hesitated, argued his ineptness, pleaded for a helper and made every excuse he could muster to avoid the burden of leadership.

But after all his hesitation and self-doubt, Moses did go and enter the land where he was an outlaw, subject to execution. There he confronted the great Pharaoh and demanded that his people be set free. The stories of the plagues which visited the Egyptians heighten the feeling of God's presence with Moses. The Hebrews' journey through the Red Sea again strengthens our conviction that the Lord was with this Moses as he sought freedom for his people.

What the biblical record only sketches, however, is the constant shadow of self-doubt that lived with Moses—his fears, his vascillations. In every discussion with the Lord,

Moses wonders, Moses doubts, Moses hesitates. In the end, Moses does act the part of the great liberator, but after long episodes of personal agony.

Faith and liberation in history

Moses the liberator is the complement of Abraham the man of faith. Faith leads to liberation. All the agony of self-doubt, all the sacrifice, all the following of inner voices urging pilgrimage, lead inevitably to a liberation from slavery. This was true for Moses who first liberated himself from the bondage of the luxury of Pharaoh's court and then liberated his people from the bondage of slave status. This is true for every person who comes to faith. Inevitably, faith will lead to a struggle for liberation.

Our lifetime has witnessed many movements which began in faith and then demanded liberation. We have seen the struggles of Martin Luther King, Jr. which brought and are still bringing liberation to black Americans. We have seen increasing numbers of young people and adults unwilling to settle for the consumer society in which we live strike out for new and different forms of life where personal freedom is more important than possessions.

We have seen great movements of political liberation in South America, movements which spring from a committed faith in the Lord. All across our world the child of faith is liberation—not merely liberation of self but a struggle for liberation of the downtrodden and the powerless.

In the long course of Christian history this is what has happened to those who have listened to and followed the call of Jesus. Believers in Jesus have been a leaven in the mass of people, demanding, urging, struggling for a greater personal freedom, first for themselves, and as they mature, freedom for the masses of downtrodden people.

To this day Jewish people revere Moses as the great liberator. Their highest yearly festival is Passover, the day of liberation from Egypt. We Christians follow in their footsteps and celebrate that Passover as an even deeper liberation, one from the bonds of sinfulness, brought by the "new Moses"—Jesus, the Christ. Our Passover is the Good Friday—Easter celebration, the most important feast in our calendar. Faith leads toward freedom.

Faith, then, is not a deadening opiate as some have charged. God's call to us should not be a drug to deaden the pain of slavery and oppression. Rather, the opposite is true. Faith is a call to liberation. Faith without liberation is sterile, pointless, ineffective. Only when this faith in the Lord leads to personal and social liberation is it fully within the historical stream of the faith of Abraham, Moses, and the Lord Jesus.

Men and women of faith are free men and women—free within themselves, free to take the risks life demands. And they are liberators who bring this inner freedom to the problems of life as Moses did. Far from being a deadening thing in life, faith is the energizing force behind many, if not all, the great movements toward freedom in our world today and in the long history of our race.

PONDERING POINT

Longing for Freedom

Like air, water, and the other taken-for-granted realities of life, freedom is seldom appreciated until it is lost. Peoples who have lived without freedom for a long period of time bear witness to the fundamental longing for it.

No people in modern times have so exemplified this longing for freedom as have the black Americans. A slave people for centuries, blacks exploded into freedom in the middle of the last century only to discover that real freedom was to be denied for yet another hundred years.

During the centuries of slavery and semi-slavery, the black American did not cease to long for freedom. In the biblical stories of escape from bondage, blacks discovered a model for their own desires. Much of the beautiful music which surfaced during these years of suffering is based on the biblical motif and the intense longing for a world in which all were free.

To recall but a few of the spirituals shows one how persistent this longing actually was. "Go down Moses," "The Balm in Gilead," "Joshua," "The Bosom of Abraham," and "Nobody Knows the Trouble I've Seen" all express this longing for a better day. All also make use of biblical characters and events to dramatize the longing.

The close kinship between the suffering black people and our biblical ancestors indicates how fundamental is the desire to be free. In a society where freedom is seldom seriously reflected upon, we might do well to hum once more the poignant spirituals as a kind of prayer of thanksgiving for our political and religious freedom.

PRIMARY LESSON PLAN

CLASS PLAN

Goal:
To show how every believer is called to freedom.

Materials needed:
1) Copies, one per group of three, of the Task Sheet provided with this program. See page 45.
2) Blank paper, pencil for each student
3) Blackboard, chalk and eraser
4) Newsprint, marking pen, masking tape
5) Bible

Methodology:
1. Using the Task Sheet, the students will study the various kinds of slavery common in the contemporary world and rank them in order of their destructiveness to people.
2. The catechist, using the material from the Model Presentation, "Free At Last," will show how Moses' faith experience led him to search for freedom for himself and for his people.

Opening prayer:
Read or have a student read "The Mission of Moses" Exodus 3:7-12.

Opening remarks:
In our last meeting(s) we talked about Abraham and the experience of personal faith. Remember how we described that personal faith as a friendship between the individual and God? Today and in the meetings which follow, we will be talking about the effects of that friendship. The first of these effects is the power of faith to urge us toward freedom.

Task sheet: *Allow about 15 minutes.*
Before we can talk about freedom we have to think a little about the opposite of freedom, slavery. We understand freedom best by knowing what freedom is not.

Break into groups of three while I give you task sheets and pencils. Look at the list of kinds of slavery and simply put them into order with the most destructive first, the second most destructive second, and so on. Be prepared to give reasons why you rank-ordered as you did. In fact, your reasons will be more important than your ordering.

Reporting: *(Keep score on newsprint or the blackboard.)*
Group 1, give us the five items you ranked as most destructive and the number of points you awarded each. Now, tell us why you ranked item _____ as most destructive.
Repeat process for all groups, keeping score.

Discussion:
a) Why are all the items on the Task Sheets forms of slavery? Does anyone disagree with any of the items? Why?

b) Why did some seem to you to be more destructive than others?
c) Let's compare the one that received the most total points with the one that received the least. What's the difference?
d) Can you think of other forms of slavery? For example?

SAVE POSTERS for the recap, Lesson 10.

Bridging:

Now that we have talked about slavery, we are ready to think about going out from slavery to freedom. The greatest story of leaving slavery and entering freedom, probably in all the literature of the world, is the story of Moses and the Israelites. After Abraham's death, his son Isaac and his grandsons left Palestine and migrated to Egypt. Maybe you remember the story of Joseph and his coat of many colors. This is the story the bible writer used to explain how the Hebrews went to Egypt. While there, they fell into disfavor with the Egyptian rulers and were reduced to slavery. The story I'll share with you today opens with the Hebrews as slaves in Egypt.

Before we begin, take a sheet of paper and write: "The most remarkable thing about the story is..." We'll share your answers after my presentation.

Presentation:

Use the material from the Model Presentation, "Free At Last."

Discussion:

a) Call on volunteers to share completions to the statement, "The most remarkable thing about the story is..." Encourage discussion.
b) Do you think you could live in slavery? Why? Why not?
c) Do you think God wants us all to be free? Why?
d) Do you think we can sometimes prefer slavery to freedom? When? Why?

Closing Prayer:

Moses and the Israelites were to wander on the desert for forty years before reaching the promised land. Moses was to die, at the age of 121, before the Jews crossed the Jordan river. This is the song of Moses which he spoke to the full assembly of the tribes.

The Song of Moses (Deut. 32:1-4, 7, 10-11)

Bible References

The last chapters of Genesis (37-50) recount the transition from Abraham to slavery in Egypt. Exodus, from its beginning to 15:21, tells the story of the deliverance from Egypt. Passages you might especially enjoy are:

Moses' Early Life	Exodus 1 and 2
A Second Version of Moses' Call	Exodus 6:2-13, 28-30 and 7:1-7
Passover	Exodus 12 (note the liturgical details)
Red Sea	Exodus 14

ALTERNATE PLAN

CLASS PLAN

Goal:
To show how every believer is called to freedom.

Materials needed:
1) Copies, one per group of three, of the study sheet provided with this program. See page 46.
2) Pencils for each group
3) Blackboard, chalk and eraser
4) Newsprint, marking pen, masking tape
5) If music is used for opening prayer, the necessary equipment
6) Bible for each group, reference books on American slavery and ghetto life.

Methodology:
1. Students will attempt a systematic study of 19th century black American slavery and/or contemporary ghetto life and compare this to what is known of the slavery of the Hebrews in Egypt.
2. The catechist will lead a discussion about these findings and help the students relate them to the material in the Model Presentation, Free At Last.

Opening prayer:
A newfound friendship with God changed the man who wrote this song from a hardened sea captain who brought slaves from Africa to America to a man of faith who spoke out against slavery. The song—Amazing Grace. (pg 43)

Opening comments:
Slavery is not a topic we think much about these days. There are no large groups of people held in bondage and deprived of their basic human rights. Or are there? Maybe we do not call it slavery anymore but there are the blacks in South Africa, the Ukranians in Russia, the Eastern Europeans, the American Indians, and the dwellers of our own ghettos. In many ways the condition of these people is like that of the Hebrews during their sojourn in Egypt. Although we call the domination of minorities by different names today, it is still very much like slavery.

Project: *Allow about 30 minutes.*

(Break into groups of three, give out study sheets, pencils and reference materials.)

For the next half hour I would like you to think about and study the slavery of black Americans during the 19th century or, if you wish, the slavery in our ghettos today. I have provided each group with a study sheet on which are several important questions about slavery.

As you answer these questions about slavery in more modern times, I also want you to try to answer them about the Hebrew slaves in Egypt. The record of the Hebrews is found in the first two chapters of the Book of Exodus. I also have several reference books about slavery in America and ghetto life to help you.

Reporting/Discussion:

(Use newsprint to save for the recap or blackboard.)

Now, let's ask each group to share their findings with us.

(After each presentation, ask questions like the following to help focus the discussion on the material from the Model Presentation, "Free At Last.")

1. If you had been a Hebrew slave, how would you have felt about the Egyptians? How would you have felt about your own people? How would you have felt about yourself?
2. When Moses came to bring freedom, how do you think most slaves would have reacted?
3. Why was Moses' experience of faith necessary for him before he could become a liberator? Why was some faith experience necessary for the Hebrews before they could seek freedom, too?

Catechist's presentation:

Here, the catechist may wish to review the Model Presentation, "Free At Last," or, if the class has not done the primary lesson, present the material for the first time. An introduction to a first time presentation: So far we have talked about slavery as a human experience and compared it to the slavery of the Hebrew people. Now let me tell you a little more about the Hebrews and Moses, their liberator.

Discussion:

Now that we have thought deeply about slavery and the Hebrews, let's try to get a better understanding of the relationship of faith and freedom.

a) Someone has said, "All freedom begins with a realization of one's own dignity." What do you think of that? Can a person be free who does not appreciate his own dignity?
b) How does the experience of faith assist a person in understanding his own dignity? (What happens to a person who has a good friend?)
c) How is our faith the foundation of our freedom, even today?

Closing prayer:

Lord, hear our prayer and let our cry come unto you.
That we may know your call to us to leave our slavery
    and become free . . . *(pause for reflection)*
That we may leave behind our sins, our selfishness,
    our lack of love . . . *(pause for reflection.)*
That we may bravely go out into the wanderings of our
    desert and there meet you . . . *(pause for reflection.)*
That we may have the courage to let others in our lives be
    free . . . *(pause for reflection.)*
That we may open our hearts to the pilgrimage your
    call demands . . . *(pause for reflection.)*

Lord, you called Moses and his people to leave behind the security of slavery and to follow you into the uncertainty of the desert life. May we who share this same call to rely only on you, have the same courage they had and willingly follow you. Amen.

The Nine Plagues

1. Nile turns to blood
2. Frogs overrun land
3. Mosquitoes
4. Gadflies
5. Cattle die
6. Boils
7. Hailstorm
8. Locusts
9. Darkness

Exodus 7:14-11:29

Amazing Grace

Amazing grace, how sweet the sound
that saved a wretch like me . . .
I once was lost, but now I'm found,
was blind, but now I see.

Twas grace that taught my heart to fear
and grace my fear relieved . . .
How precious did that grace appear
the hour I first believed.

Through many dangers, toils and snares,
I have already come . . .
Twas grace that brought me safe thus far,
and grace will lead me home.

MINI LESSON PLANS

The purpose of the ideas which follow is to provide the creative teacher with further suggestions for classroom experiences related to the original Model Presentation.

Cardinal Mindszenty

Cardinal Mindszenty remains the outstanding figure of dedication to human freedom in our century. Most teenagers today have heard little about his heroic fight against tyranny. Books and films have celebrated his life. A good source of information on this great man is The Cardinal Mindszenty Foundation, P.O. Box 11321, Saint Louis, MO 63105. While some of their materials may seem overly anti-Communist to the more liberal teacher, the dedication of the foundation to personal freedom is remarkable. A study of the Cardinal will reveal many similarities to the life of Moses.

Caesar Chavez

Caesar Chavez is the acknowledged leader of Mexican-American farmworkers. His leadership is not unlike that of Moses. A good filmstrip on his life and work is *Viva LaCausa* available from Teleketics, 1229 South Santee Street, Los Angeles, CA 90015. Most diocesan filmstrip depositories stock many of the Teleketics products. Teachers can usually borrow them for a nominal fee.

Life in the Ghetto

Ghetto life is far removed from the experiences of most middle-class, American youth. However, many of them have been assigned books like *The Autobiography of Malcolm X* or *Manchild In the Promised Land*, written during the great upsurge of black rage during the 1960's. They can be asked to give a report on these books and to lead a discussion about the economic slavery experienced by many poor Americans today.

The Campaign for Human Development

This is the agency of the American Catholic Bishops' Conference dedicated to social justice and human freedom. This agency has many publications which provide both classroom activity and general information of value to the student who wishes to study the slavery of poverty stricken Americans. Most dioceses have a local office of the Campaign or a teacher may write to 1312 Massachusetts Avenue, N.W., Washington, D.C. 20005. Allow several weeks for delivery, study, and implementation in the classroom.

TASK SHEET 2

Slavery

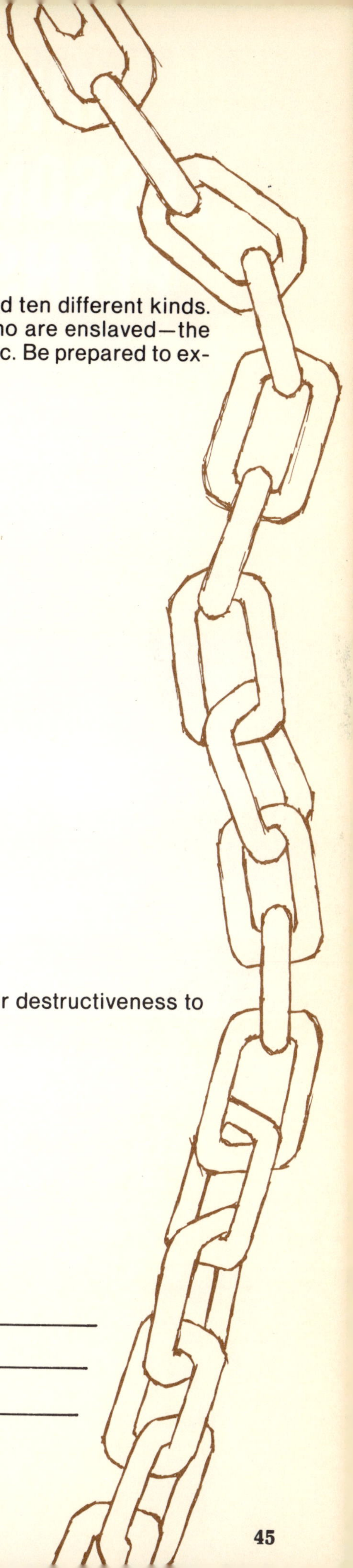

Part 1.

There are many types of slavery in our world. Below are listed ten different kinds. Rank them in order of their destructiveness to the people who are enslaved—the most destructive first, the second most destructive second, etc. Be prepared to explain your rankings.

___ A. Drug addiction

___ B. Alcoholism

___ C. Ghetto life

___ D. Retardation

___ E. Bad companions

___ F. No education

___ G. A dead-end job

___ H. A poor self-image

___ I. A tyrannical parent

___ J. A cruel friend

Part 2.

Now that you have ranked the kinds of slavery in order of their destructiveness to people, award points as follows:

5 points to the item you ranked first

4 points to the item you ranked second

3 points to the item you ranked third

2 points to the item you ranked fourth

1 point to the item you ranked fifth

NOTES: _____

_____

_____

(Duplicator master of this sheet in packet)

STUDY SHEET 2

Let My People Go

Questions

	American Slavery (19th century and/or ghetto life now	Hebrew Slavery of Old Testament
1. What was the cause of the slavery?		
2. How were the slaves brutalized? (examples)		
3. What effect did the slavery have on the slaves? (examples)		
4. Why did the masters resist freeing the slaves?		
5. Without faith, what will happen to freed slaves?		

(Duplicator master of this sheet in packet)

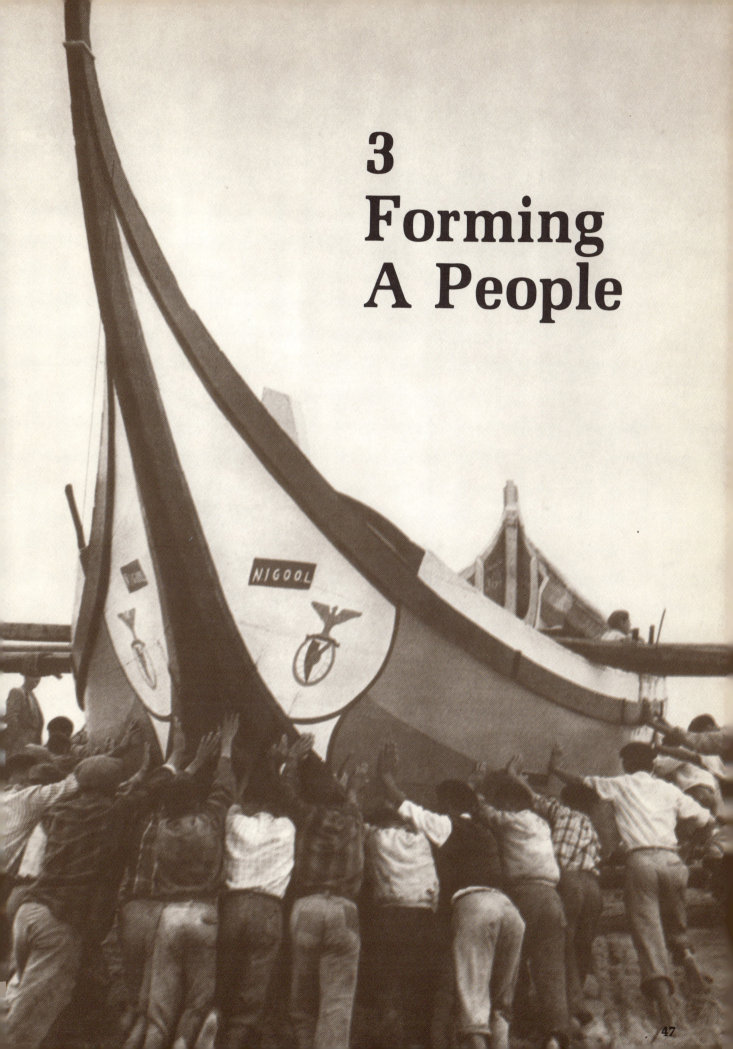

3 Forming A People

CATECHIST'S BACKGROUND

History of the covenant

The idea of a covenant was not new with Moses. When a king conquered a tribe or nation, he had a long legal document drawn up. In this document the recently defeated nation promised obedience to their conqueror. The conqueror, in turn, promised to protect the defeated from the depredations of their neighbors. This covenant contract was not the agreement between equals but rather one imposed upon the defeated by their conqueror.

Among the early Israelites the written word was seldom used. In its place the spoken word was endowed with special solemnity and public notice. Once the word had been spoken under such solemn circumstances, it might never be revoked. Even today marriage contracts are solemnized by the spoken word uttered amid great liturgical solemnity. The solemnity and public notice are for much the same purpose as they were among the ancient people.

Even before Moses the bible records covenants. Abraham made a covenant alliance with the Canaanites Eshcol and Aner (Genesis 14:13) and with Abimelech (Genesis 21:22). Isaac made a similar covenant about water rights (Genesis 26:26). Jacob, Abraham's grandson, made a covenant with Laban, his uncle, (Genesis 31:44) in which he promised to marry only Laban's daughters and in which Laban promised to respect Jacob's borders. Thus, even in Israelite history the idea of a covenant was a common one as it seems to have been among many Near Eastern peoples.

Moses' covenant

After the people of Israel had passed from bondage to freedom, a remarkable event in itself, Moses led his people to an understanding of the meaning of this event. He proclaimed to the people that the Lord had a special affection for them. They were to become a holy nation, a priestly people. In order to proclaim this in a way the ordinary Israelite could understand, Moses made use of two different liturgical ceremonies.

In the first, an altar was set up as a symbol of God. All the people were assembled before it. After sacrificing an animal, Moses sprinkled the altar and the people with the blood of this ritual victim. This symbolized that the Lord had become a blood relative with Israel, that now the members of this desert tribe were blood brothers with the Lord.

A second liturgical act is also recorded in Exodus. In this liturgy, Moses, Aaron and the 70 elders representing all the clans of Israel were seated at a solemn banquet. They ate together with the Lord and became one family with him.

These two ceremonies help the modern reader understand the depth of the covenant relationship. It was more than a mere legal contract. In fact, such covenants were considered to bestow a kind of family relationship upon those who took part in them. Next to the bonds of blood, the covenant relationship was considered the most sacred. When the one party to this special covenant was the Lord, the staggering implications of Moses' liturgical acts become clear.

Probably no amount of explanation can summon up for the modern reader the profound impact of this covenant liturgy on this recently liberated people. We have not experienced the hopelessness of slavery, the insecurity of the desert nor the sense of defeat and self-hatred which comes with such experiences. Only with these experiences as a background can one hope to grasp the wonder at the largess of the Lord which must have filled this people's hearts.

The covenant and community

Not only were individuals given a great dignity through the covenant relationship, they were related in a special way to all other covenant members. Historians tell us that the original Israelites were probably not related by blood in the way the bible stories lead one to believe. More than likely the desert wanderers were a rag-tag group of slaves from Egypt, runaway slaves at that. Few could document their relationship with a common ancestor. Moses himself may even have been an Egyptian. Yet, once the covenant relationship had been born, these people had a special relationship to one another.

This special relationship forbad all acts of injustice toward a fellow Israelite. Murder, adultery, theft, false witness, and

even the desire for these were forbidden among members of God's special people. They were to worship only the one God, to honor His name and to celebrate His special Sabbath Day. Many other regulations protected the community life from the depredations of the strong and powerful among them.

Throughout their history the Hebrew people have been conscious of this special community relationship within Israel. Interest on loans was forbidden among members of the community, one was urged to love his countryman but to avoid the alien, marriage within the covenant community was encouraged while marriage with aliens was forbidden. A whole series of customs and regulations grew up to protect the special kinship enjoyed by all who were children of the covenant.

The New Covenant

Christians, from the beginning, understood their own special relationship with the Lord Jesus as a covenant relationship. They thought of Jesus as the priest and the victim. Through his death on the cross all were bathed in his blood and thus all made blood kin with him. The final meal with his disciples was the inauguration of a new covenant, just as the desert meal had been the symbolic inauguration of the old covenant.

This new covenant conferred upon Christians a sense of community, an obligation to treat all fellow Christians as Jesus had treated them. The special bond of relationship was not a common ancestor but a common faith in Jesus as Lord. Saint Paul even spoke of this special interrelationship among Christians as one of a single body so intimate and so profound was it.

To be a Hebrew, then, was to live within the community formed by the covenant, to respect the other members of the covenant and by one's own life to foster the covenant relationship. To be a Christian is also to live within the community formed by the new covenant, to respect and love all other members of that group and to foster the health of the community by the goodness of one's own life. For both old and new covenants, community is the natural and inevitable outcome of a special relationship with the Lord.

Pedagogy

In this lesson we have focused on the importance of community within Israel and in the Church today. The **Primary Lesson Plan** asks students to think about different kinds of groups and to distinguish among them. This leads the catechist to a presentation of the nature of covenant community as explained in the **Model Presentation.** The **Alternate Lesson Plan** suggests a visit to a religious community and a discussion of the strengths and problems of community living.

The **Mini Lesson Plans** suggest an overview of the books of the Old Testament, a filmstrip study, a study of the Amish people, and a familiarity with the work of Saul Alinsky, whose community building efforts are very important in many cities in the U.S. today.

The **Catechist Resource Sheet** contains a list of all the books of the bible, some comments on their content and an explanation of the two different lists or canons of books popular among Christians and Jews today.

MODEL PRESENTATION

"Forming A People"

Topics to be presented:

1. Once free, the Israelites looked for a purpose for their freedom.
2. The covenant they made in the desert gave them this purpose, community.
3. Today's believers still seek community to balance their freedom.

Freedom's limitations

Out in the desert free from Pharaoh and his slavemasters, the first blush of liberation swept over the Hebrew people like the warm rays of a summer dawn. They were exuberant, full of life and song. Miriam, Moses' sister, led them in a mighty war chant recorded in the Book of Exodus. Liberation meant joy.

But soon the burden of being free began to weigh heavily on the shoulders of these ex-slaves. What about bread? What about meat? When they were slaves someone had provided these elements of life for them. Being free meant that they had to provide for themselves in a desolate land. Was freedom worth the struggle? Wasn't it easier to return to the land of bondage than to press on through the endless desert toward this mythical land of milk and honey? Wasn't Moses a trickster who had talked them into exchanging their chains for something worse—insecurity?

These were the thoughts and feelings of the men and women of Israel as they marched through the dry desert wastes of Sinai. Three times they neared revolt, once about bread, once about water, once about better food. Moses, with the genius of a great leader, sensed the problem. These were men and women free only **from** something, not yet free **for** a cause, not yet proud of their freedom.

Covenant Community

In the midst of the desert wastes, even before ending the pilgrimage in the land of promise, Moses began the task of forging nationhood, of building up a sense of interdependence so the people would depend not on the overlords of Egypt but on one another.

The bible records the great liturgies of the desert wandering which were Moses' way of dramatizing the emergence of the new nation from the ashes of its enslaved past.

In the greatest of the liturgies Moses mounted a hilltop to build an altar, a symbol of the Lord. There on that altar he placed a calf, itself a symbol of human strength, and in a

53

priestly gesture, slew the animal. As the blood ran from the dead carcass, Moses had it scooped up and sprinkled on the altar. This showed in symbol that human strength belonged to the Lord. That was the usual way of doing things.

But then in a dramatic move, he took some of the blood and had the people sprinkled with it. They were sprinkled with the same blood as the altar. Symbolically they knew they were now blood brothers with this strange Lord who set their pilgrimage in motion. They were a new people, not just this man and this woman, not just people bound together by some common ancestry, but now blood brothers and sisters with the Lord and with one another.

This sense of kinship has served Jewish people well. For centuries they have had no national location but continued their sense of kinship with one another—God's own people, brothers and sisters all.

The desert liturgies of Moses dramatize an element of our faith experience. Like Abraham, we hear the inner urgings of faith and, like Moses, are called upon to liberate not only ourselves but our burdened brothers. Yet, like Moses and the Hebrews this liberation is strong stuff. We sense the need to share our experiences of freedom with those who, like us, know freedom. We sense the need for what theologians call community.

Community makes it possible to live in freedom. Without it, life is too complicated for the ordinary free person. It is so much easier to leave the dry edge of the desert and retreat into the bondage of slavery.

Community today

When we come to faith, perhaps during a retreat, during a crisis of conscience, or through a family problem, we know the liberation of faith's force in our lives. But soon, maintaining that fervor becomes a heavy burden. We know the weariness of the Israelites wandering in the desert. The promised land seems so far away—so distant. How can we maintain the force of faith and freedom in an alien land?

The answer today is the answer Moses knew four thousand years ago—community. Believers need believers. There is no substitute. We all need people who have experienced faith as we have, people who can understand what it is we mean when we talk of freedom. These people need not be of our age group or even of our nationality but they do need to be of our faith experience.

Perhaps the greatest struggle of our young years is the struggle to find others who believe as we believe. A religion class can open up possibilities. The local parish may contain some who believe as we do. School is rife with possibilities but, in the end, the struggle to build a faith community is a difficult one.

The difficulty in building such a community does not excuse the believer, however. For without a community of faith, fervor cannot last very long.

PONDERING POINT

Searching for Community

The search for faith community is as old as Israel and as new as tomorrow. Throughout the Old Testament there is evidence of small groups of men and women who went apart to discover in one another the true meaning of covenant and faith. The Books of Kings tells us of the sons of the prophets, small subcommunities in Israel based on fervent faith. Both Elijah and Elisha were said to have such companions.

Toward the end of the Old Testament era recent history has uncovered the remnants of the Essenes, a group of believers who retired from Israel in order to live more dedicated lives.

Christianity itself followed this pattern. As early as the third century groups of monks settled in great numbers in Egypt. Here they followed a strict monastic discipline and discovered in their mutual companionship a true Christian community.

Saint Benedict was the first in the West to organize such attempts to find community. His monasteries dotted the landscape of every European land and later gave birth to a flowering of religious communities of many kinds including the Franciscans, the Dominicans, the Trinitarians, and many others. All had in common the desire to build a community among those who took faith with an uncommon degree of seriousness.

In North America today communities of Charismatics bear witness to a continued desire to live the dedicated community life. Marriage Encounter communities, missionary communities, communities bound to serve the urban poor, and a plethora of others all indicate the desire for faith in community is very much alive.

PRIMARY LESSON PLAN

CLASS PLAN

Goal:
To show how all believers need community.

Materials needed:
1) Copies, one per group of three, of the Task Sheet provided with this program. See page 61.
2) Blank paper, pencil for each student
3) Blackboard, chalk and eraser
4) Newsprint, marking pen, masking tape
5) Bible

Methodology:
1. Using the Task Sheet, the students will discuss different kinds of human groups and try to understand the "glue" which holds them together.
2. The catechist, using the materials from the Model Presentation, "Forming A People," will describe how Moses led the Hebrews into community, a deep-seated human need for all who will be free.

Opening prayer: (Isaiah 57:14-15, 18-19)

Open up, open up, clear the way,
remove all obstacles from the way of my people.
For thus speaks the Most High,
whose home is in eternity,
whose name is holy:

"I live in a high and holy place,
but I am also with the contrite and humbled spirit,
to give the humbled spirit new life,
to revive contrite hearts.

I will heal him, and console him,
I will comfort him to the full,
both him and his afflicted fellows,
bringing praise to their lips.
Peace, peace to far and near,
I will indeed heal him," says the Lord.

Opening remarks:

We have talked now about Abraham and the experience of faith and how that faith led Moses to search for freedom for himself and for his people. But, that was not the end of Moses' story. Freedom apparently was not enough—for being free is such a lonely experience without others to share it with. To help the Hebrews preserve their freedom, Moses set about the work of building a community of free believers.

Task sheet:

But, before we talk about Moses we ought to try to understand why people form groups—whether they are little cliques at school or great nations like the United States or Canada. We need to grasp why different groups of people feel at home with one another. This will help us understand more deeply what Moses was about.

Break into groups of three while I pass out the task sheets and pencils. *(Read the directions.)* Any questions?

Allow about 15 minutes.

Reporting: *(Use newsprint or the blackboard.)*

A. First let's look at Part 1 on our task sheet. What "glue" holds a street gang together? *(Call on groups for answers and list them.)* What about a nation? *(Repeat process as above for each item listed on the task sheet.)*
B. Let's move on to Part II, then we'll have some general discussion of groups. What do all the groups have in common? *(Call on groups for responses; list them.)*

Discussion:

a) How many of the "glues" we listed do we find in the large group we call Christians? The group we call the Roman Catholic church?
b) What happens to a group that loses its "glue"?
c) Do you think being a member of a group limits your freedom or helps you have more freedom?

SAVE POSTERS for the recap, Lesson 10.

Bridging:

Now that we have some understanding of why groups are groups, we can look to Moses and see how he formed a group (community) from people who had little in common except their escape from Egypt.

Before we begin, take a sheet of paper and write: "The Hebrews needed to form a group because...". After my presentation, we'll share your responses.

Presentation:

Use the material from the Model Presentation, "Forming A People."

Discussion:

a) "The Hebrews needed to form a community because..." *(Call on volunteers for responses. Encourage discussion.)*
b) What do you think would have happened to the Hebrews if they had not formed a tight group?
c) What did the followers of Jesus do after his death and resurrection? Why did they do this? What would have happened if they hadn't formed groups?
d) The church is often referred to as a community of faith. Why?
e) What do you think would happen to your faith if you never came in contact with others who believe as you do? Why?

Closing prayer:

Read or have a student read: (Psalm 146:2, 7-10.)

Sacrificial Offerings of the Hebrew Community

1. burnt offerings (whole animal is destroyed)
2. cereal offerings (grain)
3. peace offerings (re-establish friendship with God)
4. sin offerings (to obtain forgiveness, usually for sin against God)
5. guilt offerings (to obtain forgiveness, usually for sin against neighbor)

Bible References

Exodus 16-35 recounts the Hebrew desert wandering and their covenant with the Lord. Of special interest are:

Israel's Revolt	Chapters 16-17
The Covenant	Chapter 24
The Golden Calf	Chapter 32

ALTERNATE PLAN

CLASS PLAN

Goal:
To show how all believers need community.

Materials needed:
1) Blackboard, chalk and eraser or newsprint, marking pen, masking tape, for formulating questions before the visit.
2) Permission slips, if required.

Methodology:
1. The catechist will present or review the material from the Model Presentation, "Forming A People," and help the students formulate questions for their visit to a religious community.
2. The students and the catechist will visit a community and discuss the benefits of community life with members.
3. The catechist will help the students reflect upon the experience.

Note:
To obtain the maximum benefit from such an experience, the catechist should arrange for a period of reflection before the trip and some time for reflection after it.

Advance preparation:
1. Several weeks before the lesson the catechist should choose an existing local community and make arrangements for a visit by the class. Monastic communities are ideal for such a visit—Trappists, Benedictines, Visitation Sisters, etc.
2. Before going, be sure to arrange with the community for the opportunity to see the place and to discuss community life with one or more members of the community. This discussion is the more important part of the experience. If a trip is impossible, the catechist might bring a community member to the class for a discussion. But, the total effect of the trip—the visit and the discussion on the "home turf" of the community—will be more effective.
3. The catechist should also check with the principal or coordinator to be sure such a trip is permissable in the school or CCD setting and observe whatever formalities (permission slips, insurance, transportation regulations, etc.) are required.
4. Arrange transportation and supply students with detailed schedule.

Before the visit

Arrange for a half-hour meeting of the class in order to discuss what questions the class will ask the community.

Here, the catechist may wish to review the Model Presentation, "Forming A People," or, if the class has not done the primary lesson, present the material for the first time. From the insights in the essay about the necessity of community, help the students see the parallel between the religious community they will visit and the community of Israel in the Old Testament.

The following are suggested questions:
- What benefits do you derive from being members of your

community? Why would a person join you in this kind of life?
- What sort of things does your community do together?
- What kinds of signs and symbols do you use to show to yourselves and others that you are a community?

Compile your own list and bring it with you to the interview. Appoint a member of the class to take notes during the visit for use in reflecting on the experience and for the Lesson 10 recap.

During the visit

First, try to get a good picture of the physical setting of the community. Allow the students as much time as possible to poke around and savor the experience. Students are likely to ask many questions, some of which may seem too personal to the catechist. But it is better for the catechist to fade into the background and allow the community member to establish his or her own relationship with the students.

Second, try to arrange a semi-formal meeting with a community member in some setting like a livingroom, common room, etc. Ask the students to present the questions they worked out in advance. Once again, the catechist should attempt to set up a dialogue between students and community member and then to be as retiring as possible under the circumstances.

After the visit

On the way home, possibly in a restaurant or at the parish center or school, try to arrange a period of reflection together. The following questions may help stimulate some discussion:

1. What did you think was the most important thing you experienced during the visit? Why?
2. How was this group similar to the Hebrews? How dissimilar?
3. Why do you think people still want community?
4. How does community presuppose faith? What has faith to do with founding a community?

Prayer suggestions: Community (Acts)

These remained faithful to the teaching of the apostles, to the brotherhood, to the breaking of bread and to the prayers.

The many miracles and signs worked through the apostles made a deep impression on everyone.

The faithful all lived together and owned everything in common; they sold their goods and possessions and shared out the proceeds among themselves according to what each one needed.

They went as a body to the Temple every day but met in their houses for the breaking of bread; they shared their food gladly and generously; they praised God and were looked up to by everyone. Day by day the Lord added to their community those destined to be saved. (Acts 2:42-47, The Early Christian Community.)

Brotherly Love (Psalm 133)

How good, how delightful it is
   for all to live together
   like brothers:

fine as oil on the head,
   running down the beard,
running down Aaron's beard
   to the collar of his robes;

copious as a Hermon dew
   falling on the heights
   of Zion,
where Yahweh confers
   his blessing,
   everlasting life.

MINI LESSON PLANS

The purpose of the ideas which follow is to provide the creative teacher with further suggestions for classroom experiences related to the original Model Presentation.

The Jewish Bible

The Jewish Bible or in Catholic terms, the Old Testament, is the record of the community of Israel and the inspiration for its continuance. On page 62 is a list of the books, the abbreviations used for them, and some short bits of information about them. This list can provide the teacher with a tool to use as an overview of the whole Old Testament. The introduction to each of the books in the *Jerusalem Bible* or *Dictionary of the Bible* by John L. McKenzie, The Bruce Publishing Company. Milwaukee, Wisconsin, will provide ample background information for a presentation.

A Film and a Filmstrip

Baptism and *Blessed Are the Parkmakers* are two aids which will make happy additions to the study of community. *Baptism* is a 16 mm. film in which a young orphan boy finds acceptance in a community of his peers, and *Blessed Are the Parkmakers* is a filmstrip which leads the students into a community simulation. Both are available from Teleketics, 1229 South Santee Street, Los Angeles, CA 90015, or from your diocesan film depository.

The Amish

The Amish are one of the few existing religious communities which are large enough to be studied extensively. Students might be asked to research several topics centered on Amish ways such as: Amish Women, Amish Education, Amish Church Services, Amish Fathers, etc. Librarians in the local public library will help students locate relevant books and magazine articles. During the student presentations, the teacher should draw out the similarities between the Amish and the early Hebrews.

Community Development

Community development is a concept familiar to most Americans. Saul Alinsky was the guiding spirit of this movement, although by no means the only practitioner. Most cities of any size have professional community developers at work among ethnic and neighborhood groups. Students would profit from an opportunity to discuss modern community development and to see how similar this work is to the task undertaken by Moses.

TASK SHEET 3

Community

There are many different groups of people. But, behind every group lies a reason why these individuals spend time together or at least think of themselves as one group. Below are listed several different kinds of groups. Try to discover the "glue" which binds them together.

Part 1

Group	Glue
A. A street gang	_____
B. A nation	_____
C. A family	_____
D. The soda shop crowd	_____
E. An army	_____
F. A school club	_____
G. A football team	_____
H. A recreation center	_____
I. A class in school	_____

Part 2.

What things do all the above groups have in common? _____

_____

_____

_____

_____

_____

(Duplicator master of this sheet in packet)

CATECHIST RESOURCE SHEET

The Books of the Bible

The Pentateuch or the Law

(These five books contain myth, history and tribal recollections but only as the setting for the law.)

Genesis (Gn)	Adam, Abraham, Isaac, Jacob, and Joseph
Exodus (Ex)	Moses, Freedom, Covenant, Desert wandering
Leviticus (Lv)	Laws and some history
Numbers (Nu)	Laws and some history
Deuteronomy (Dt)	A second telling of exodus, laws

The History Books

Joshua (Jos)	Entry into Palestine
Judges (Jd)	Early warrior heroes
Ruth (Rt)	A tale of a valiant woman
I, II Samuel (I S, II S)	Samuel, Saul, David
I, II Kings (I K, II K)	Solomon to the captivity
I, II Chronicles (I, II Ch)	Other stories from the same era.
Ezra (Ezr)	Rebuilding Jerusalem
Nehemiah (Ne)	Rebuilding Jerusalem
Tobit (To)	A tale of heroism in captivity
Judith (Jdt)	A tale of feminine heroism
Esther (Est)	A tale of faithfulness
I, II Maccabees (IM, 2M)	Later Jewish history—2nd cent B.C.

The Wisdom Books

Job (Jb)	An inquiry into the problem of suffering
Psalms (Ps)	Prayers for all situations of life
Proverbs (Pr)	Maxims to live by
Ecclesiastes (Qo)	Also called Qoheleth, reflections on life
The Song of Songs (Sg)	A beautiful love poem
Wisdom (Ws)	Poems in praise of wisdom and the good life
Ecclesiasticus (Si)	Also called Sirach, sayings about the good life

The Prophetic Books

The major prophets

Isaiah (Is)	Warnings, theology, reasons for hope
Jeremiah (Jr)	Warnings and a call to repentance
Lamentations (Lm)	Poems attributed to Jeremiah
Baruch (Ba)	Poems and prophecy
Ezekiel (Ezk)	Warnings, calls to repentance
Daniel (Dn)	Stories with a message for persecuted people

The minor prophets
Hosea (Ho), Joel (Jl), Amos (Am)
Obadiah (Ob), Jonah (Jon), Micah (Mi)
Nahum (Na), Habakkuk (Hab), Zephaniah (Zp)
Haggai (Hg), Zechariah (Ze), Malachi (Ml)

The two lists

Most Protestant Bibles and most Jewish Bibles do not include the following books in their list of canonical (authentic) books:

I, 2 Maccabees, Tobit, Judith, Sirach (Ecclesiasticus), Wisdom, Baruch, and parts of Daniel and Esther. These books are called deuterocanonical by Catholics and the apocrypha by Protestants. The controversy over these books goes back to Jewish thought. Palestinian Jews accepted only books written in Hebrew while non-Palestinian especially those from Alexandria in Egypt accepted some few books written in languages other than Hebrew. Catholics followed the Alexandrian canon probably because it was translated into Greek, a language most could understand. Later, Protestants, in a desire to rediscover the primitive church, settled on the purer Palestinian canon.

4 The Lawgiver

CATECHIST'S BACKGROUND

The purpose of law

In the Spring of each year, Americans celebrate Law Day. On that day, learned speakers explain to audiences which already believe the importance and the sacredness of all human law. Meanwhile the busy public largely unaware of the learned discussions goes about the business of creating new law, changing outmoded law, and establishing the consensus on which the entire legal system is built.

Many North Americans mistakenly believe that law originates in the houses of government and springs from the wisdom of the legislators. In fact, this step in the formulation of law is one of the last moments in the birth of any legislation. Long before a subject can be introduced into a governmental debate, a long process of preparation must begin in the informal daily lives people live.

All law begins with an idea. Ideas themselves are usually the result of an experience. When many people in a society have had a new and different experience, one person will verbalize the meaning of that new experience. As the group begins to understand what the new experience means, it often changes its way of thinking and acting. Slowly a new custom takes form. Later, often much later, legislators formulate that new custom into what we today call law. The process of moving from experience to idea, to custom, to law is a complicated and lengthy one. Because it is so complicated and lengthy, people usually invest their laws with a sacred dimension to insure that their collective wisdom will not be easily changed.

The Israelites experienced faith, freedom and national community in the desert. This experience gave birth to the idea of the covenant. Moses verbalized this idea and taught it to the people through his impressive liturgies. Once grasped, this covenant ideal formed the basis of new behaviors and so of new customs. In time these customs were officially proclaimed as law by kings, priests and other officials. Still later these laws were written down and given a sacred character.

As we today look back over the process of lawmaking we may tend to be disillusioned. For us as children law seemed to have a magical source, to be outside human experience, to be imposed on humankind from above. As we become aware that law is more human than we once believed, we can make the mistake of losing our respect for it or our sense of its sacredness. The contrary should be the case, for law as we have it both in the bible and outside it is sacred. It does come from God through the mediation of His finest creation, the human mind. Rather than something imposed arbitrarily upon unthinking masses of people, law is the result of the collective wisdom of generations of good men and women in search of a decent way of living.

The history of Israel's law

During this century archeologists have discovered several codes of law which are much older than the law of Moses. All of these codes originated in the same part of the world as did the bible law. Among the discoveries are two which go back beyond the time of Abraham himself, the codes of Lipit-Ishtar and Eshnunna. There is also the famous Code of Hammurabi written about the time of Abraham, the Hittite and Assyrian laws written after Abraham but before Moses. All of these laws are similar to the law we discover in the early books of the bible.

These similarities among ancient laws lead scholars to believe that the peoples of the Near East had developed a series of traditions and customs which governed their daily lives. They had long ago decided that killing was forbidden, that marriage was to be respected, that property had to be protected, and that untruth destroyed the fabric of civilization. In simple, concrete ways the various peoples made these basic insights operative in daily life.

The Mosaic code shares with other Near Eastern laws the same basic principles but there are differences. In the Hebrew tradition the experience of covenant looms large over all law. Jews obey the law because it is a covenant responsibility. The law is not merely the accumulation of human wisdom. It is the will of their own God. Obedience to the law brings not only peace and order, it brings the mercy of the Lord. Breaking the law not only invites the penalties of the community, it brings the displeasure of the Lord and even His punishment. In Israel the sacred character of the Law takes on a new importance.

Legal problems

As one begins a study of the many laws in the early bible books, he or she is struck by their profusion, the different solutions to the same problems, and the existence of laws governing a settled agricultural society interwoven with laws that obviously belong to a much earlier age. These problems demand some rational explanation.

Scholars distinguish six different codes of law in the first five books of the bible. Each of these codes undoubtedly arose to meet the needs of a sector of Israel at a different time in its history. Yet, because all law was seen as part of the covenant experience, these codes were interwoven into the great covenant narrative. To highlight their importance several miraculous and wondrous stories were added to introduce these

laws to the reader. These wondrous stories were important not for their truth or lack of it but as signs that the laws which followed were indeed a part of the will of the Lord first expressed in the covenant experience.

The Ten Commandments are the shortest of these codes, probably the most ancient, although in the form we have them they do not come from the time of Moses. This code is contained in two different versions in the bible (Exodus 20 and Deuteronomy 5), which leads scholars to believe that an earlier and simpler law once existed, one in which all the regulations were as simply stated as are the prohibitions of murder, adultery and false witness.

In the Ten Commandments is a code of conduct suitable for all times. Later codes attempt to concretize this law to meet the changing situations of a developing society. With the development of social consciousness these primitive laws demanded amplification and change. Jesus himself took these laws to new depths of meaning. He said of himself that he had not come to change the Law but to bring it to its own fulfillment.

For reasons like these, Christians today still revere the Ten Commandments, but in their interpretation of them have added new understandings and new insights born of the experience of living not in the old covenant but in the new.

Pedagogy

The **Primary Lesson Plan** presents students with a practical problem of developing their own law. The **Model Presentation** explains to the class how Moses and his followers confronted the task of bringing order and tranquility to Hebrew society. The **Alternate Lesson Plan** asks students to study a modern novel which demonstrates as do few others the necessity of custom and law for a decent life.

The **Mini Lesson Plans** suggest a study of some Church laws, a filmstrip study, a discussion with a rabbi, and a task oriented group discussion.

The **Catechist Resource Sheet** contains several Canon Laws for use with the Mini Lesson Plan on that topic.

MODEL PRESENTATION

"The Lawgiver"

Topics to be presented:

1. In order to preserve their freedom and build their community, the Israelites needed law.
2. All good law is sacred because all human life is holy.
3. The Ten Commandments, the core of Israel's law, protect freedom and community.

Law and freedom

We have studied Moses the man of faith. We have seen how his faith led him to seek freedom for himself and his people. In our most recent lesson we studied how Moses protected that freedom by building a community. Today we will spend one final lesson on Moses. In this lesson we will talk about another important contribution of Moses to his people, his concern for law.

Moses knew with the intuition of any great leader that freedom and community without law meant no more than license for the powerful and new oppression for the little people. He knew what any historian can easily prove that most revolutions bring freedom only for a short time. They are usually followed by a new tyranny. We know that this was true in Russia where the people were no sooner liberated from the Czar than they were once more tyrannized by the Communists. We know that this was true in France during the Revolution. People overthrew the monarchy only to be tyrannized once more by the terrifying orders of the Revolutionary directorate. History tells us quite clearly that only law protects the little people from the tyranny of the powerful.

What has always been true for humankind was true for Moses and his people in the desert. He wanted freedom and community to last, to become a part of the Hebrew tradition and not to be lost in some new tyranny as bad or worse than that of the Egyptians. To preserve freedom and build community Moses gave his people law.

Law's sacredness

This law of Moses was so important to the writers of the Book of Exodus that they described its birth in vivid and dramatic stories. Moses was portrayed as a kind of minor god. When he gave Israel its law he was surrounded by fire and lightning. His voice echoed like the desert thunder. He wrote not on paper or clay but on stone. These laws were so important and so crucial to the life of Israel that Hebrew stories gave them an almost supernatural beginning.

What the authors of Exodus were trying to tell their

readers was that these laws were sacred and should not be changed. Even today we know that good law is sacred because human life is holy. Whatever protects life and freedom, whatever builds community is the work of God Himself.

Many of the flourishes in these stories of the birth of Moses' law are, then, literary devices. The importance and the sacredness of the law were heightened by these flourishes, whether for the unthinking reader who takes them at their face value or for the more sophisticated one who knows that the flourishes are a frame used to emphasize the essential picture, the law of Moses and his people.

The Ten Commandments

These laws of Moses are basic to human life even today. First, there is the command to worship one God and to respect His name. The community of Israel existed because of the freedom faith gave to it. To lose faith is to lose freedom, at least eventually. Men and women can be free and treat others as free only when they believe there is a reason for this, a reason more important than their petty selfishness. With the loss of belief in a God who cares about each person comes a loss of respect for the rights of the powerless and the consequent destruction of freedom. Every act of worship of God, then, is an affirmation of human freedom.

But, how does one worship? For Moses and his people it was through prayerful rest on one day of each moon's quarter. This day was dedicated to the Lord, to prayerful contemplation of the wonders He had done and to rest. How few people think even today of the necessity of rest and the contemplation rest can bring for the preservation of human freedom. Only when people reflect on their faith experience and its meaning in changing times can freedom be held intact.

And then, there were the basic rights of every man and woman—their life, their family, their property and their good names. In a series of rapid-fire commands Moses summed up the roots on which human freedom rests. When one member of the community feels free to violate these rights, no one is free.

Today in our community of faith which we attempt to form with others who share our experience of God, these commands still hold true. We can live comfortable in a community only when we are certain that no one in that community will deprive us of what is basic to our personalities—our lives, our possessions as an extension of our personalities, our good names as necessary for our personalities to grow, and our families as the creative culture in which our personalities are rooted.

Conclusion

Moses, then, was a great person. His deep faith experience led him to freedom. He found ways to share that freedom with his fellow Israelites. From this rag-tag group of former slaves he fashioned a community with God at its head, a community in which it was possible to maintain faith and so freedom. Finally, he gave that community a law, something to insure that even the powerless could be truly free. Jewish people see Moses as the greatest of their leaders. Christians rank Moses only less than Jesus himself. He was at once the great visionary and the practical man of freedom's affairs.

PONDERING POINT

Law and Freedom

Many Catholic Americans see in the law of the Church an impediment ot their personal freedom. Church law is seen as an endless list of do's and don't's with little purpose other than to establish order and keep the laity docile.

It comes as something of a surprise to those who feel this way to learn that one of the most progressive forces in the reform of the Church has been the American Canon Law Society. This group of professional Church lawyers has been in the forefront of efforts to liberalize Church legislation and to safeguard the fundamental rights of individuals.

Many are aware that the Church's law on granting marriage annulments has changed enough to permit thousands who were unable to marry within the Church to do so now. This struggle to discover ways of maintaining the sanctity of marriage and still protect the good conscience of individuals has been one of the most significant achievements of this group.

Other areas of concern to these lawyers have been the laicization of priests, the rights of the laity in the parish council movement, the dispensation of sisters from their vows, and many other topics fraught with public controversy. In each case, the society has stood firm for the protection of the rights of individuals and so shown the value of law not only as a protection of the community but as a bullwark for the rights of individual Church members.

PRIMARY LESSON PLAN

CLASS PLAN

Goal:

To show how all who live in community need a law.

Materials needed:

1) Copies, one per group of three, of the Task Sheet provided with this program. See page 77.
2) Pencil for each group
3) Blackboard, chalk and eraser
4) Newsprint, marking pen, masking tape
5) Bible

Methodology:

1. Using the Task Sheet, the students will try to form a code of conduct suitable for a group of teenagers marooned on a deserted island.
2. The catechist, using the material from the Model Presentation, "The Lawgiver," will show how Moses gave the Hebrews a law to live by and show, too, why that law was necessary.

Opening prayer:

Blessings on those who keep God's commandments.

Read Leviticus 26:3-13, pausing for reflection between verses.

Opening remarks:

We spoke about Abraham at the beginning of this unit. Remember how we dwelled on his faith experience? In the past few meetings we have been discussing two of the effects of the faith experience—freedom and community. Today we will look at another of faith's effects—law. Law is necessary in order to preserve community. As almost everyone knows, Moses was the great lawgiver, the one who put order into the life of Israel.

Task sheet:

Before we turn to Moses, let's see if we can do in a limited way what Moses did for Israel. Break into groups of three while I pass out the task sheets and pencils. Your task is to imagine that you are marooned on a deserted island and need some kind of law to live by. See what you can do with your law and be prepared to give us reasons for your decisions. Any questions?

Allow about 15 minutes.

Reporting:

(Use newsprint or blackboard.)

A. Now let's look at Part 1. I'll call on each group and ask you to give us one of the laws you made and why you thought the law was necessary. *(Repeat this process until you have a good list.)*

B. In part 2 you were asked who most needs laws and why. Who will share your answer with us? *(Call on volunteers and list reasons.)* Does anyone disagree with any of these reasons? Why?

Discussion:

a) What do you think would have happened if the group had decided to leave everyone free and had made no laws? Explain.
b) Did you find it difficult to think of laws? Why?

SAVE POSTERS for the recap, Lesson 10.

Bridging:

Now that we have seen how difficult it is to form laws even with the experience of living in a very sophisticated civilization, we can understand the gargantuan task Moses had as he tried to find the right words and the right laws for a tribal people who had only just learned what it was to be free.

Presentation:

Use the material from the Model Presentation, "The Lawgiver."

Discussion:

a) What impressed you most about what I just said? Why?
b) Does this discussion of Moses and the law help you understand why churches, nations, and even families have to have law to live together? Why?
c) What is the law of Jesus? How is it different from the law of Moses? How is it similar?
d) What three things have we talked about that follow the experience of faith? Why are they necessary?

Closing prayer:

(Psalm 1:1-3)

Happy the man
who never follows the advice of the wicked,
or loiters on the way that sinners take,
or sits about with scoffers,
but finds his pleasure in the Law of Yahweh,
and murmurs his law day and night.

He is like a tree that is planted
by water streams,
yielding its fruit in season,
its leaves never fading;
success attends all he does.

Bible References

Exodus 16 through 40 is filled with references to the law. So, too, is the whole Book of Leviticus and much of Deuteronomy. Of special interest are:

The Ten Commandments	Exodus 20 and Deuteronomy 5:1-21
The Covenant Code	Exodus 20:22 to 23:33
The Ritual Commandment	Exodus 34:17-27
The Holiness Code	Leviticus 17 through 26

ALTERNATE PLAN

CLASS PLAN

Goal:
To show how all who live in community need a law.

Materials needed:
1) Three copies of "Lord of the Flies" by William Golding
2) Blackboard, chalk and eraser
3) Newsprint, marking pen, masking tape

Methodology:
1. The students will study William Golding's "Lord of the Flies" as a parable of man without law.
2. The catechist will lead a discussion about the law and review or present the material from the Model Presentation, "The Lawgiver."

Advance preparation:
Recruit three students to read and report to the class on the short book, "Lord of the Flies." Since this book is popular in high school English classes, you might well have several students who have already read this modern classic.

Ask one student to tell the story from the vantage point of Ralph, the young man who tried to impose an English order upon island life.

Ask the second student to tell the story from the vantage point of Jack, who led another group with a very different idea of law and island order.

Finally, ask the third student to tell the story from the vantage point of Simon, the hero of the story, who dies a tragic death.

Opening prayer:
Read or have a student read the Ten Commandments.

Opening comments:
Writers have always been fascinated by desert islands. Whether it is Robinson Crusoe or Swiss Family Robinson or a score of lesser books, the theme is the same—civilized people without the force of law. The question is, how well will people cope with life when removed from their law and the order of their daily lives.

One modern book about desert islands and lost people is William Golding's "Lord of the Flies," an account of a group of choir boys who were cast up on a desert island with no adult supervision. This book is the story of their attempt to find order and create civilization in the midst of many misadventures.

Reports:
I have asked _____ to read this short book and tell the story as best he/she can from the vantage point of Ralph the young man who tried to impose an English order upon island life. When _____ finishes, you may ask him/her questions about the details of the story.   *Allow 10 minutes.*

I also asked _____ to read the same book and to tell the story from the vantage point of Jack, who led another group with a very different idea of law and island order. When he/she finishes, you may also question him/her. *Allow 10 minutes.*

Finally, I asked _____ to read the book and to tell the story from the vantage point of Simon, the hero of the story, who dies a tragic death. His understanding of island order will be very different from that of the other two. *Allow 10 minutes.*

Discussion:

If we as a group were on that island, how do you think we would have coped with the situation? *(If you did the task sheet for the primary lesson, recount some of the suggestions.)*

Catechist's presentation:

Here, the catechist may wish to review the Model Presentation, "The Lawgiver," or, if the class has not done the primary lesson, present the material for the first time. An introduction to a first time presentation:

The Hebrews were much like people marooned on a desert island. They had left all the law and order of the past in Egypt to form their new community in the desert. But, all communities have problems. These problems demand solutions. Moses was a pragmatic man as well as a deeply religious one.

Discussion:

(Record the important ideas on newsprint or the blackboard.)

Now that we have thought about the choir boys on the island and about Moses, let's see if we can understand why there was law in the Old Testament.

(You may want to list the Ten Commandments before this discussion.)

1. What do you think of the Ten Commandments as a simple guide for life together as a community? What are its strengths? What are its weaknesses?
2. If you had to add one commandment to this list, what would it be?
3. If you had to drop one commandment, what would it be? Why?
4. Do you think most people today obey the Ten Commandments? Why? Why not?
5. Which of the Ten Commandments do you think is violated most today? What effect does this have on the community?

SAVE POSTERS for the recap, Lesson 10.

Closing prayer:

This is the Ten Commandments written in a more modern style, expressing the same laws in a way we today can easily understand.

O Lord, help me live the law of love. May you be first in my life with nothing there before you. May I speak of you with tenderness and use my tongue always for your praise. Let my knees bend in solemn worship on your day and my heart be filled with kindness toward those who first gave me life. And, let me never harm another whether through my strength of limb or through my desire for power over man or woman. May I speak with perfect honesty and great care for other's reputation. And finally, may I never desire the blessings you in your wisdom have given to my brothers and sisters but be content with the life you have laid out for me. Amen.

Israel's Law:

... rested on authority of God
... blended civil and religious rules
... was the same for all
... had fixed penalties

The Ten Commandments

1. I am the Lord thy God; thou shalt not have strange gods before Me.
2. Thou shalt not take the name of the Lord thy God in vain.
3. Remember thou keep holy the Lord's day.
4. Honor thy father and thy mother.
5. Thou shalt not kill.
6. Thou shalt not commit adultery.
7. Thou shalt not steal.
8. Thou shalt not bear false witness against thy neighbor.
9. Thou shalt not covet thy neighbor's wife.
10. Thou shalt not covet thy neighbor's goods.

MINI LESSON PLANS

The purpose of the ideas which follow is to provide the creative teacher with further suggestions for classroom experiences related to the original Model Presentation.

Canon Law

Although few Catholics think much about it, the Catholic Church has a codified law. While this code of laws is now under revision, it remains the official law of the church. On page 78 are several selections from this code. Students may be asked to find biblical passages which remind them of these selections. The teacher may also want to invite a priest skilled in canon law to explain the topic to the class.

Filmstrip Study

A series of four filmstrips called *Old Testament Life and Times* by Family Films and available through Roa Films, 1696 North Astor Street, Milwaukee, WI 53202, or your diocesan film depository, presents the customs of the Hebrew people which were later codified into law. This series divides these customs into the nomad life, city life, military and political life, and religious life. The viewing will take some time but will give students a background to Jewish law they may not find in any other resource.

Invite A Rabbi

Invite a rabbi to the class to discuss the different attitudes toward the Law common among Jews today. A rabbi is trained to know the Law and the many interpretations of it. Students might also profit by planning a visit to a local synagogue and/or attending an actual Sabbath service. Further information on Jewish belief and custom is available in *World Religions For the Classroom*, Dorothy Dixon, Twenty-Third Publications, P.O. Box 180, West Mystic, CT 06388. While this book is written for teachers of intermediate level children, it is filled with fascinating information and projects many high schoolers could enjoy.

A Good Discussion

A worthwhile topic is, "If you had to eliminate one of the Ten Commandments, which one would it be and why?" In championing different points of view students come to see the necessity of all ten. You may also change this by asking "If you had the opportunity to add one commandment to the traditional ten, what would it be? Show how this is not covered by one of the ten." This discussion will lead to a better understanding of the comprehensiveness of the traditional list.

TASK SHEET 4

The Island

Suppose you are members of the school Spanish Club making a trip to Latin America to study the Spanish language firsthand. On your flight there, your plane has engine failure, crashes and kills all the adults on board. The students manage to swim to a deserted island where you do not expect to be sighted or rescued.

After a few days of chaos, everyone comes together to try to organize life on the island by making some laws to live by.

Part 1.

List the five most important laws you would make.

1. _____
2. _____
3. _____
4. _____
5. _____

Part 2.

Who do you think would need these laws the most and why?

_____
_____
_____
_____
_____
_____
_____

(Duplicator master of this sheet in packet)

CATECHIST RESOURCE SHEET

Selections from Canon Law

Just as the ancient Jewish people governed their lives together by law, so do present day Catholics. Our official law is called the *Code of Canon Law*. This compilation of over two thousand laws was given to the church by Pope Pius X and Pope Benedict XV in 1918. It is presently being revised but continues as the official church law.

The following are some extracts which may be of interest to the teacher and to students, especially if discussed within their historical contexts.

The Duties of a Pastor (canons 467 and 468)

The pastor must celebrate the divine services, administer the sacraments to the faithful as often as they lawfully ask for them, know his parishioners, prudently correct those who go astray, embrace in his paternal charity the poor and distressed, and employ the greatest care in the Catholic education of children.

The pastor must with zealous care and abundant charity assist those in the parish who are ill, especially those who are near death, solicitously comforting them with the sacraments and commending their souls to God.

Indulgences (canon 911)

An indulgence is the remission before God of the temporal punishment due for sins whose guilt has already been forgiven, granted by ecclesiastical authority from the treasury of the church, by way of absolution for the living and by way of suffrage for the departed.

Marriage (canons 1012, 1013, 1039, 1070, 1094)

Christ Our Lord, elevated the very contract of marriage between baptized persons to the dignity of a sacrament.

The primary end of marriage is the procreation and education of children; its secondary end is mutual help and the allaying of concupiscence.

Ordinaries of place [bishops] can forbid marriage in a particular case, but only temporarily and for a just cause and as long as such cause continues, to all persons actually stopping in their territory, and to their subjects even outside their territory.

A marriage contracted by a nonbaptized person with a person who was baptized in the Catholic Church or who has been converted to it from heresy or schism is null.

Only those marriages are valid which are contracted before the pastor or the Ordinary of the place, or a priest delegated by either of these, and at least two witnesses.

Church Bells (canon 1169)

It is proper that every church should have bells with which to call the faithful to divine services and other acts of religion. Church bells, too, should be consecrated... The use of church bells is subject exclusively to ecclesiastical authority.

Burial (1203)

The bodies of the faithful deceased must be buried; and their cremation is reprobated.

Sunday Mass (canon 1248)

On feast days of obligation Mass must be heard: and one must abstain from servile work, from judicial proceedings and... from public trafficking, public gathering of buyers and sellers, and all other public buying and selling.

5
The Voice of Discontent

CATECHIST'S BACKGROUND

History of the period

Israel did not emerge from the desert a completely formed nation. In fact, Israel remained not a unified nation but a confederation of tribes for 200 years after the conquest of the Promised Land. The period from 1260 to 1040 B.C. was spent in a slow process of subduing the inhabitants of the Promised Land, developing customs and institutions and learning again and again the meaning of the covenant experience. Only in 1040 B.C. was this people ready for the kingship of David and Solomon.

During these eventful two centuries each of the 12 tribes maintained its separate life. Each struggled against neighboring enemies, developed its own customs and had its own leadership. Once each year, we believe, leaders of all the tribes met at the shrine at Shiloh where the ark of the covenant was preserved. Here they reaffirmed their covenant with the Lord and with one another. Except for this loose confederation (technically an amphictyony), there was little national life in Israel.

Local leaders during this period were called judges. They were both men and women. Their own force of personality and success in warfare rather than any inherited position gave them the positions they held. They remained in positions of leadership during their own lifetimes and were remembered by later generations through folk tales, ballads and other forms of verbal tradition.

The religious life of Israel during these two centuries was also fragmented. Several shrines developed. In each of these, local priests attempted to keep alive the great desert days of covenant with the Lord. As they did so, each shrine developed slightly different traditions and a literature of its own. Our earliest source for the Pentateuch (the J source) probably dates from a shrine in southern Palestine during this period. It is probable that these shrines kept alive the stories of the judges until a later chronicler was able to collect and unify the entire story.

The moral life of the community of faith during these years was still primitive. We read that the judge Jephthah offered his own daughter in ritual sacrifice. We note that Samson was something of a philanderer and that extermination of the enemy was seen, in some cases at least, as a sacred duty.

Under the pressure of a newcomer to Palestine, the Philistines, the confederation grew more and more cohesive. As the Philistines conquered the entire Mediterranean seacoast and extended their sway into the fertile valleys of Galilee, the Hebrew confederation reorganized itself into a monarchy. The last of the great judges, Samuel, provided the king and the days of Israel's innocence were at an end.

The theology of Judges

The Book of Judges is anything but subtle. The writer proclaims that there is a pattern in history. First, the people forget their covenant responsibilities and fall into worship of local gods. As a punishment for this behavior God sends conquerers to enslave and degrade them. Chastened by this punishment, the Hebrews turn once more to the Lord and reaffirm their dependence upon Him. Once God is assured of

His people's conversion, He sends a leader to rescue them from their enemy and restore them to freedom and dignity once more. This pattern is reenacted over and over again, not in one tribe but in each of them. Fourteen stories of such sin and redemption are told in the Book of Judges.

The First Book of Kings completes the history of this era with several stories of the last and the greatest of the judges, Samuel. Samuel alone of all the judges achieved national recognition. He was accepted as a leader by all the tribes. This probably happened because of the dire political and military situation brought on by the expansion of the Philistines. Under this pressure the confederation quickly united and gave up its prized tribal life in exchange for the security and safety a monarchy promised.

Judges as literature

In American folklore, the stories of the great cowboy heroes come close to the tales of the judges. In these stories the enemy is totally evil and the hero completely dedicated to the good of his people. Like the cowboy stories, the judges are men (and women) who bring freedom to the oppressed and then disappear from the scene. It is the courage and achievement of a single person which is celebrated in both the stories of the cowboy and the judge heroes.

The first of the major judges was a woman named Deborah. With the aid of a hesitant soldier, Barak, Deborah destroyed the army of Jabin, the king of Canaanites. In this story the writer is at pains to point out that Deborah acted not on her own but as an instrument of the Lord. The Canaanites were equipped with ironclad chariots while the forces of Barak were on foot. At the crucial moment, however, the writer tells us that the Lord struck terror into the hearts of the Canaanites. The victory, then, is the Lord's. Chapter 5 of the Book of Judges retells the story of Deborah in a beautiful poem, probably one that was sung in a local shrine to commemorate her victory.

Another of the early judges was Gideon. The writer of Judges tells an elaborate story of Gideon's selection by the angel of the Lord to liberate his people. In this story the role of God is even more explicit than in the story of Deborah. Here, the Lord deliberately reduces the size of Gideon's army so that when victory comes all will know that it was the Lord who conquered the enemy.

The last of the stories in Judges is a cycle of tales about the legendary Samson. In this series of tales the writer of Judges had undoubtedly relied on several folk tales current at his time. His own rendering of them, however, makes the power of the Lord shine through the earlier legends and become the explicit mover of Israelite victory.

In The First Book of Samuel the narrative of this period of history comes to an end. Samuel is the acknowledged leader of all the tribes of Israel. With his blessing and the Lord's power, Israel embarks upon the final cleansing of the Promised Land. Samuel anointed and later removed the first king, Saul, from office because he had failed in his devotion to the Lord. This was the final act of a theological age in which no human power counted more than the power of the Lord. In the age of kings which followed, the identification of the king with the religious leadership of Israel broke the simple purity of a complete dependence upon the Lord for the daily preservation of a never too secure society.

Pedagogy

In this lesson we have highlighted the importance of dissent in religious history. This dissent from the customs of the time is embodied in the judges, in Samuel, and later in the prophets. In the next lesson we will highlight the nation builders, David and Solomon.

The **Primary Lesson Plan** discusses the role of public criticism in community life. The **Model Presentation** shows the role of the judges in purifying Israel from its mediocrity and tepidity. The **Alternate Lesson Plan** suggests the viewing of a filmstrip on Samuel.

The **Mini Lesson Plans** contain lessons which spring from filmstrip viewing, a study of the cowboy story, a role playing experience, map making, and a study of newspaper articles.

MODEL PRESENTATION

"The Voice of Discontent"

Topics to be presented:

1. After its desert days Israel often forgot its covenant with the Lord.
2. The Judges recalled Israel to its first fervor.
3. The community of faith must always be recalled to its ideals.

Faith grown cold

Today we will talk about a topic all of us know quite well—human laziness. Because of our laziness, faith and freedom and even community and its necessary law have a way of growing cold. These great realities of life become taken-for-granted and are often almost forgotten. Their inner urge is ignored and only the words remain. Organization tries to replace community and law inhibits the freedom it was supposed to nourish. Such is the way of history in this world of lazy men and women.

And so it was with Israel. With all its energies expended by its triumphant entry into the Promised Land, with its great discovery of freedom in the desert long forgotten and its understanding of the purpose of its law grown dim, men and women turned back to lives of humdrum slavery. This time their slavery was not to Egyptian masters but to local superstitions. As the people of Israel forgot God, they were easy prey to local pagan armies and soon were conquered once again. True to His covenant, God did not forget His people. He once more liberated them from their enemies and reestablished them in freedom, community, liberty, and law. He did this through a series of heroic men and women called the Judges.

The Judges

The stories of these liberators are recounted in the Book of Judges. The stories are among the most primitive in the entire bible. Undoubtedly they began as campfire tales, were set to music as ballads and later found their way into the liturgies of religious festivals. Finally, they were written down and incorporated into the bible. These always colorful stories tell a simple theme. That theme is: when Israel forgot God it fell into slavery from which God once again liberated them through the judges.

The first of the great judges was a woman, Deborah. She saw her people oppressed by Jabin, king of the Canaanites. The bible writer notes that this domination by the Canaanites was just payment for their forsaking the heritage of Moses and their fathers. Deborah rallied the men of Israel and routed the forces of Jabin. Even Jabin's proud general Sisera, perhaps a king himself, found death at the hands of a peasant woman. She drove a wooden tent peg through his head as he lay sleeping after his defeat by the armies of Israel.

And, there is Ehud who assassinated the Moabite king, Eglon. He gained access to the king by deceit and then pulled out his hidden dagger. So violent was the thrust of his concealed weapon, the bible account read, that the hilt was buried in the rolls of fat in the king's stomach. A strong story! But, beneath the gore and violence is another liberation of Israel, another call to covenant and law.

There are also Gideon and Jephthah and the memorable Samson. And there are the names we seldom hear—Abdon and Elon, Ibzan and Tola, Jair and Shamgar. In each case, the judge not only brought political deliverance but more importantly, recalled Israel to the purity of its original desert experience.

The last and the greatest of these early leaders of Israel was Samuel, a prophet whom the biblical writer calls the last of the judges. As a young boy Samuel came to study in the sanctuary of the Lord. There he had a unique faith experience which led him first to prophesy and then to witness the destruction of his people's oppressors, not foreign dignitaries this time but priests of their own nation. Samuel called and recalled his people to live the community of faith and to observe the freedom and law of Moses.

Samuel was profoundly mistrustful of organization in the life of his people. He knew how easily organization could take the place of faith and community. When the people asked for a king to rule over them, Samuel refused to sanction any monarchy. He resisted organization because he foresaw, and foresaw correctly, that this monarchy, when it would lose its life of faith, would destroy liberty and pervert community into nationalism and law into power.

In the end, however, Samuel gave in and initiated the monarchy but only because the people demanded it. He refused to sanction the idea that Israel could have any loyalty other than a loyalty to the Lord.

Constant recall

The Judges and Samuel represent a strain of thought which continued through the prophets up to and perhaps including Jesus himself—the recall to the ideals of Moses and Abraham, faith, freedom, community, and law. Theirs were the dissenting voices, the anti-establishment cries for justice, the insistent calls to reformation.

All through Christian history, too, such voices have been heard. There was Francis of Assisi, John Bosco, Mother Cabrini, and in our own day, John XXIII—all voices crying in the wilderness, calling for return to the ways of our pristine past.

Not all believers must follow this route. Nor can all believers be expected to take the message of these mighty people with complete literalness. But, the theme of their message—community not organization, faith not religion, freedom not slavery, law not manipulation—remains the perennial call to all who share the faith experience of Abraham, Moses, and the Lord Jesus.

PONDERING POINT

The Labor Movement

When American history is summed up by historians writing long after the nation has expired, scholars will give great attention to the American Labor Movement. It has influenced our society more than any other movement and may well be the principal force in preserving it.

At the end of the last century Americans took it for granted that a few people should control the nation's wealth. The divine right of kings did not exist here but the divine right of business leaders did. Churches blessed the aggressiveness of business leaders, novelists celebrated their success, and governments stood or fell at their pleasure. Radical revolutionaries alone called for some limitation on their power.

Into this taken-for-granted order of things, came the tiny American Labor Movement. It raised a voice, often strident, at times vitriolic, demanding a reform and a return to the ideals contained in the American ideal. In its age the Labor Movement was the prophetic voice, the voice of discontent.

Today our American society is very different from what it was 100 years ago. That difference has not been brought about by bloody revolution but by the constant struggle of the little people through the Labor Movement. Labor unions may today be more aggressive than is good for some sectors of society. They may fail to represent the most needs. Yet, in the big picture, the picture seen by centuries, they have been the great voice of reasoned reform in our land and to them Americans owe a great debt. Without them this land would most likely have known bloody revolution.

PRIMARY LESSON PLAN

CLASS PLAN

Bible References

The whole Book of Judges and the first fifteen chapters of I Samuel contain the history of this period. Interesting passages are:

Deborah and Barak	Judges 4 and 5
Gideon	Judges 6, 7, and 8
Samson	Judges 13, 14, 15, and 16
Samuel's Call	I Samuel 3

Goal:
To show that living in community demands a critical stance.

Materials needed:
1) Copies, one per group of three, of the Task Sheet provided with this program. See page 93.
2) Blank paper, pencil for each student
3) Blackboard, chalk and eraser
4) Newsprint, marking pen, masking tape
5) Bible

Methodology:
1. Using the Task Sheet, the students will discuss when public criticism is helpful and when it is not helpful for the community.
2. The catechist, using the material from the Model Presentation, "The Voice of Discontent," will present the Judges and Samuel as voices raised in opposition to the over-organization of Israel.

Opening prayer: (I Samuel 2:2, 6-9)

More than anything Hannah, who was fast growing old, wanted a son. She promised that she would give him to Yahweh for all his life. To the amazement of all, Hannah did bear a son, Samuel, who was to be one of the great critical voices of Israel. Our opening prayer is called The Song of Hannah, a prayer of thanks to Yahweh for Samuel (1 Samuel 2:2, 6-9).

Opening remarks:

Last time we concluded our study of what happens when a group of people become believers. Remember the three consequences of faith: freedom, community and then law. Today, and in our next topic, we will be talking about how you live in that free community with its law. Communities, be they villages or nations, have a way of growing stale, of losing their first fervor. They have a way of getting too organized and forgetting why they came to be in the first place.

Task sheet: *Allow about 15 minutes.*

Today we will be talking about some men and a woman who raised their voices against this tendency to live routine lives. But before we turn to history, let's look at the present. Break into groups of three and look at this week's task sheet. (Pass out sheets and pencils.) On it are several stories of boys and girls who are critical of the system. After each story you are asked to indicate whether you think they are helpful or not helpful to the larger community. Be sure and think about the reasons for your decisions.

Reporting: (Use newsprint or the blackboard.)

VOTES

	Helpful	Not helpful
Abe	_____	_____
Betsy	_____	_____
Cal	_____	_____
Dinah		

(Call on groups in turn and keep score.)
Group No. _____, tell us what you decided about Abe and explain your reasons. *Repeat process for Betsy, Cal, and Dinah.*

Discussion: SAVE POSTERS for the recap, Lesson 10.
a) What was the most important difference between the people we thought were helpful and the ones we thought were not?
b) Do you think we all have a duty to be critical at times? Why?
c) How can we decide when to go ahead and criticize and when to keep quiet?
d) Can you think of examples of people who are critical and their criticism is helpful to all of us?

Bridging:
Now that we have talked about the voices of criticism and discontent in our lives, let's look to some of the remarkable people in the early years of the Old Testament, the Judges. They were the critics of their time, the left wing if you will, who spoke out against the status quo and demanded a return to the faith of Moses and Abraham. Before we begin, take a sheet of paper and write: "We, like the ancient Israelites, need voices of criticism because . . ." After my presentation, complete the statement and we will discuss them.

Presentation:
Use the material from the Model Presentation, "The Voice of Discontent."

Discussion:
a) What impressed you most about what I just talked about?
b) Do you imagine the Judges were liked by the Hebrew people? Why? Why not?
c) Who will volunteer a completion of the statement: "We, like the ancient Israelites, need voices of criticism because . . ."
d) Does Jesus remind you of the Judges? In what way?

Closing Prayer: (Psalm 71:1-8)

In you, Yahweh, I take shelter;
never let me be disgraced.
In your righteousness rescue me, deliver me,
turn your ear to me and save me!

Be a sheltering rock for me,
a walled fortress to save me!
For you are my rock, my fortress.
My God, rescue me from the hands of the wicked,
from the clutches of rogue and tyrant!

For you alone are my hope, Lord,
Yahweh, I have trusted you since my youth,
I have relied on you since I was born,
you have been my portion from my mother's womb,
and the constant theme of my praise.

To many I have seemed an enigma,
but you are my firm refuge.
My mouth is full of your praises,
filled with your splendour all day long.

The Song of Hannah

There is none as holy as Yahweh,
(indeed, there is no one but you)
no rock like our God.

Yahweh gives death and life,
brings down to Sheol and draws up;
Yahweh makes poor and rich,
he humbles and also exalts.

He raises the poor from the dust,
he lifts the needy from the dunghill
to give them a place with princes,
and to assign them a seat of honour;
for to Yahweh the props of the earth belong,
on these he has poised the world.

He safeguards the steps of his faithful
but the wicked vanish in darkness
(for it is not by strength that man triumphs).

ALTERNATE PLAN

CLASS PLAN

Goal:
To show that living in community demands a critical stance.

Materials needed:
1) Copies, one per student, of the reaction sheet provided with this program. See page 94.
2) Pencil for each student
3) Projection equipment and filmstrip (See advance preparation below.)
4) Bible

Methodology:
1. Students will view a filmstrip describing the life and times of Samuel and, as they do, fill in a reaction sheet.
2. The catechist will lead a discussion which will focus on the material from the Model Presentation, "The Voice of Discontent."

Advance preparation:
Several weeks before this class the catechist will have to arrange for:
(1) a filmstrip projector
(2) a record player
(3) a projection screen
(4) a person familiar enough with the machines to run them without creating a crisis in the class
(5) a copy of either:
Samuel: Kingmaker of Israel (50 frames, 17 minutes)—part of "Heroes of Israel, Stories from the Old Testament" by Cathedral Films, P.O. Box 1608, Burbank, California 91507. (Art)

-or-

Samuel, A Dedicated Man—part of the Old Testament Scriptures by Concordia Publishing House, 3558 South Jefferson Ave., Saint Louis, Missouri 63118. (Live characters)

Opening prayer:
(Wisdom 9:1-5, 7, 9-10, A Prayer for Wisdom.)

God of our ancestors, Lord of mercy,
who by your word have made all things,
and in your wisdom have fitted man
to rule the creatures that have come from you,
to govern the world in holiness and justice
and in honesty of soul to wield authority,
grant me Wisdom, consort of your throne,
and do not reject me from the number of your children.

For I am your servant, son of your serving maid,
a feeble man, with little time to live,
with small understanding of justice and the laws.
You yourself have chosen me . . .
to be judge of your sons and daughters.
With you is Wisdom, she who knows your works,
she who was present when you made the world;
she understands what is pleasing in your eyes
and what agrees with your commandments.
Despatch her from the holy heavens,
send her forth from your throne of glory

to help me and to toil with me
and teach me what is pleasing to you.

Opening comments:

Sometimes we think that dissent is a modern invention, something that began in the 1960's, and that up until that time everyone agreed what should be done. Well, the history of Israel gives lie to such a mistaken impression. Almost from the beginning, there were two strains of thought in Israel.

The first strain of thought went something like this—conform, obey, do what you are told and everything will work out all right. This kind of thinking, important for the unity of Israel, was present in Moses, David, and most of the kings, priests, and official leaders.

The second strain of thought, however, was quite different. It went something like this—let's think things through before we get ourselves in over our heads. Let's not obey too quickly, for our first obedience is always to the Lord. Let's beware of men who think they can do our thinking for us.

Filmstrip/reaction sheet:

Today we will be watching a filmstrip about the life and times of one of Israel's greatest critics, Samuel. As you watch this filmstrip I would like you to fill in the reaction sheet I have given you. After everyone has filled out the sheet, we will discuss our answers.

Allow about 30 minutes for the filmstrip and reaction sheet.

Discussion:

Let's see how you answered the questions on the reaction sheet. *(Call on volunteers, solicit reactions to each response.)*

Catechist's presentation

Here, the catechist may wish to review the Model Presentation, "The Voice of Discontent," or, if the class has not done the primary lesson, present the material for the first time. An introduction to a first time presentation:

Now that we have seen the life of Samuel on film and reacted to it, let me add a few important reflections.

Closing prayer: (Selections from Ecclesiastes 3:1-8.)

There is a season for everything, a time for every occupation under heaven:

A time for giving birth,
a time for dying;
a time for planting,
a time for uprooting what has been planted.
A time for knocking down,
a time for building,
a time for tears,
a time for laughter;
a time for mourning,
a time for dancing.
A time for keeping silent,
a time for speaking,
a time for war,
a time for peace.

Bible References

1-2 Samuel relates the founding of the Israelite monarchy by Samuel and the lives of King Saul and King David.

Major parts:

1 Samuel stories (1 Sam. 1-7)
2 Samuel & Saul (1 Sam. 8-15)
3 Saul & David (1 Sam. 16-31)
4 David (2 Sam. 1-20)
5 Appendixes (2 Sam. 21-24)

Judges of Israel

Major Judges

Othniel
Ehud
Deborah
Barak
Gideon
Abimelech
Jephthah
Samson

Minor Judges

Shamgar
Tola
Jair
Ibzan
Elon
Abdon

MINI LESSON PLANS

The purpose of the ideas which follow is to provide the creative teacher with further suggestions for classroom experiences related to the original Model Presentation.

Cathedral Films

Cathedral Films has several historical filmstrips which can help students achieve a sense of the era of Judges and Samuel. Their **Stories from the Old Testament 5,** has filmstrips on Joshua, Gideon and Samson. Cathedral Films is located at P. O. Box 1608, Burbank, CA 91507. Many of their filmstrips are in diocesan film depositories.

Cowboy Stories

Stories of the West are traditional in American culture. An interesting class can be achieved by rewriting one or more of the biblical judges stories as television cowboy stories. Just add horses, the western twang, and make the enemies a band of outlaws. In fact, these primitive stories are very similar in tone and form to the American "horse opera."

Role Play

Role playing is always a good teaching technique. There are two instances in the life of Samuel which make easy role-play situations. The first is the call of Samuel recounted in 1 Samuel, chapter 3, and the dialogue between Samuel and the people over the selection of a king recounted in chapter 8 of the same book. Students can be encouraged to add details, have the characters think aloud, provide some conflict, etc., to bring out the high drama of both incidents. A similar role play might well be done with the story of Samson, recounted in Judges 13-15, or the story of Ruth in the book by that name.

Map Making

Students can be asked to prepare a map of the twelve tribes of Israel during this period of their independence. Good bibles or a biblical atlas available in most libraries will provide the model. The teacher may then wish to discuss with the students the similarity between this era in Israel's history and that of the newly independent American colonies during the period of the Articles of Confederation. Maps of the colonies will show striking similarities to the tribal map.

Newspapers

Newspaper publication for voices of dissent may be another interesting project which will allow the students to savor the importance of the critical voice in society. They can easily gather several critical points of view on ecology, politics, church life, local issues, etc. and publish these together with the ideas of Samuel in a small newspaper.

TASK SHEET 5

The Critics

Listed below are stories of people with critical attitudes toward the way life is organized around them. After reading each story, decide whether the critic in the story was helpful or harmful to the society in which he lives.

Abe is a member of the school biology club. He is very interested in biology, especially underwater life. He resents the frivolous attitude of some of the members and wants the club to expel all those who do not show up for all meetings. He reasons that this is not a social club; it is a biology club and should be taken seriously.

Abe's critical attitude is ___Helpful   ___Not helpful

Why? _____

Betsy is a member of student council and is upset by a school rule forbidding smoking in the lavatories. She reasons that people should be free to make their own decisions about smoking and not be policed as if they were juvenile delinquents or young children.

Betsy's critical attitude is ___Helpful   ___Not helpful

Why? _____

Cal is a member of a fraternity which will not accept Jewish members. He has threatened to resign unless Jewish boys are not only allowed to be members but are invited into membership.

Cal's critical attitude is ___Helpful   ___Not helpful

Why? _____

Dinah is currently a candidate for cheerleader. School policy says that only girls may be cheerleaders. Even though she is certain of being elected to the cheerleading squad, she has stated that unless at least one boy is elected she will not be a member. Otherwise, she says, cheerleaders are just sex symbols, not real leaders in the school.

Dinah's critical attitude is ___Helpful   ___Not helpful

Why? _____

(Duplicator master of this sheet in packet)

STUDY SHEET 5

Reaction Sheet

Directions: As you view the filmstrip, answer the following questions:

1. What do you think were the strengths of Samuel's character?
   _____
   _____

2. What do you think were the weaknesses of his personality?
   _____
   _____

3. Do you think Samuel should have selected a king when he was so opposed to the idea? Why?
   _____
   _____

4. If Samuel had really wanted a king, do you think he still would have chosen Saul?
   _____
   _____

5. What part of the filmstrip impressed you most? Why?
   _____
   _____

6. What picture impressed you most? Why?
   _____
   _____

7. Does Samuel remind you of anyone in our modern world? Who?
   _____
   _____

After viewing the filmstrip, I'd like to know more about...
_____
_____
_____

(Duplicator master of this sheet in packet)

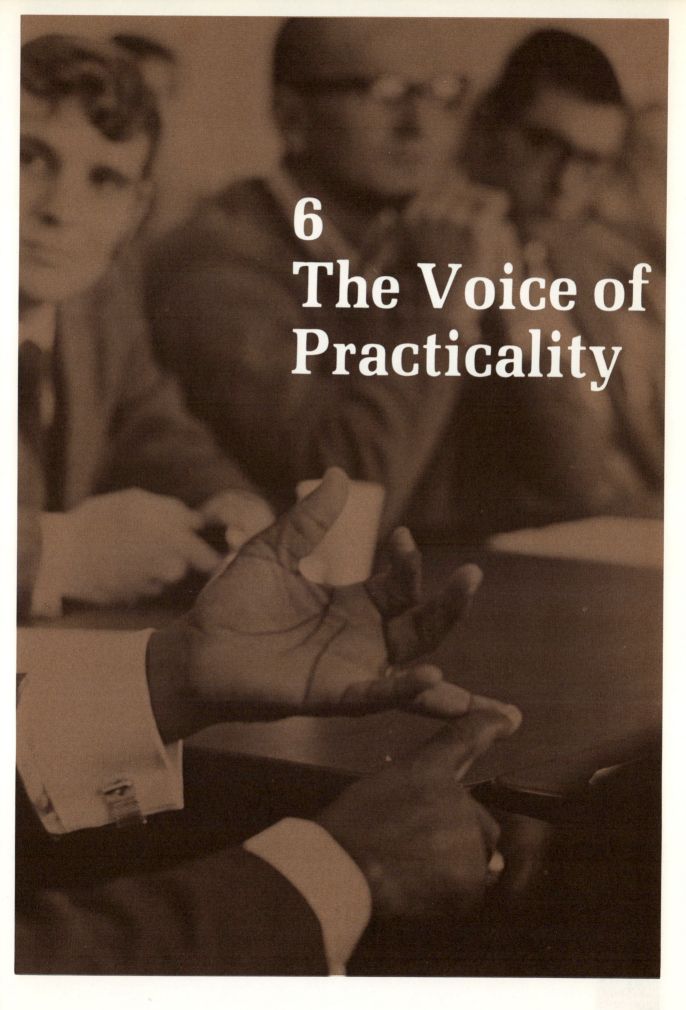

6
The Voice of Practicality

CATECHIST'S BACKGROUND

David's rise to power

Israel's transition from a loose confederation of tribes to a unified kingdom was a turbulent one. At the beginning of David's life Israel existed much as it had since the days of Joshua, a loose federation of independent tribes moving rapidly toward an at least temporary nationhood. By the time of David's death Israel was a unified kingdom which extended far beyond the original tribal lands, had its own national capital in Jerusalem, and was regarded as a powerful state in the Near East. This transition was largely the work of David.

Scholars believe that David may not have even been an Israelite by birth but that his father's family was welcomed into the confederation during the desperate days of the Philistine invasion. Whatever the truth of this assumption, David was chosen to lead the Israelites by the aged Judge, Samuel. Saul, Samuel's first choice as king, had refused to obey the oracles of the Lord and so was to be replaced. David's anointing by Samuel took place quietly. The first half of his life was spent waiting for the proper moment to assert his latent kingship.

As a young boy David entered into Saul's service. One story tells us David was the court musician, another that he slew the Philistine hero, Goliath. Soon David's fame rivalled Saul's. Saul reacted to David's growing popularity by banishing him from the kingdom under the threat of death.

For several years David lived the outlaw's life. During this time the stories seem to tell of David's close association with the Philistines, Israel's enemy. They granted David a small fiefdom in southern Judah which he defended as the Philistines themselves definitively conquered Israel and killed both Saul and his son Jonathan.

After Saul's death, David was accepted as king by the two southern tribes, Judah and Benjamin. The 10 northern tribes remained faithful to Ishbaal, another son of Saul. For several years the two kingdoms were at war with each other. Only when Ishbaal insulted his own general, Abner, did Abner betray the northern kingdom into David's hands. At last David was the king of all 12 tribes. From a poor shepherd boy, he had passed from court musician, to outlaw, to king of his people.

David the unifier

Shortly after becoming king of the 12 tribes, David chose a city on the border of the two kingdoms as the site for his royal capital. He sieged the fortress city and captured it. This city became Jerusalem, the national center for Hebrew life during the lifetime of David and his son Solomon.

To the new capital David brought the ark of the covenant, long in disuse among the Israelites because of its failure to protect them from the Philistines. As David brought the ark into the city, he danced with such exuberant joy that his wife, Michal, was embarassed by his enthusiasm. For her disloyalty Michal was banished from the royal bedroom for the remainder of her life.

In Jerusalem David built a royal palace, a spendid building by the standards of those days. This was the first public building in Israelite history. Here David set up his friends as chieftans and counselors. Here he issued edicts for forced military service and forced labor. Here he organized the wars which extended the kingdom to the mountains of the north, the deserts of the south and the wilderness east of the Jordan River. Here he set up the civil service which was to blossom in Solomon's reign.

The kingship

With David, Israel entered into a new understanding of itself and its role. The king in Israel, as in all ancient cultures, was understood as a mystical embodiment of all the people. What he did and what was done to him happened to the entire people. The king's sins were the sins of the nation writ large. The king's virtues were the virtues of his people.

As Israelites entered into this new form of thought, the importance of the individual was lost for a time. The stark realism of the desert and the age of Judges gave way to a cloudy mysticism of the royal era. People may have grumbled about their enforced labor, their taxes or military service but knew or thought they knew that obedience to the king was obedience to the Lord.

The security needs of this struggling people had forced them to exchange their individualism and tribal structure for the monarchy. Samuel, the last of the judges, had warned them of the consequences of such an act. Even the Lord was reported to be opposed to this development. As the age of kings played out its history of petty wars, unbridled luxury and religious formalism, the Lord sent his prophets to awaken Israel to a knowledge of the true spirit of the nation. It was only the pressure created by these voices of dissent which kept Israel from becoming no more than another Oriental despotism.

The rule of David, then, marked a new phase of Israel's life. This phase was both good and bad. It brought greater security and power to Israel but at a price of individual freedom and responsibility.

David as a symbol

For later Israelites David became a symbolic figure. He was the first member of a dynasty which would last forever. That dynasty would provide an ultimate liberator of Israel from her oppressors. In the course of this symbolic development of the king, the idea of a messiah arose. This messiah was to be David's descendant and, like him, to rule over the pagan nations as well as all of Israel. He was to usher in an era of peace as David had, a time when each person might recline under his own arbor and enjoy tranquility.

With the strange paradox of which history is replete, the warrior and lusty despot became the symbol of the coming prince of peace. The psalms, themselves symbols of the highest Israelite piety, were attributed to David although few could have been written by him. The unity won by David was so prized by later generations of his people, they were able to overlook his gross behavior and terrifying faults and see in him a symbol of all that was best in their tradition.

It was this summation of the best of Israelite history in the person of David that served and still serves as a symbol of Jesus.

Methodology

In the previous lesson we showed the importance of the discontented voice in the formation of authentic community. In this lesson we will emphasize the contrary but complementary voice, the one of practicality and unification. David will be our symbol of this ideal.

The **Primary Lesson Plan** asks students to work with their own parish council on the problems of the young as a counterpoint to the lesson which went before. The **Model Presentation** shows David as the unifier of Israel. The **Alternate Lesson Plan** is an extension of the primary plan and involves the youth in an actual dialogue with parish council members.

The **Mini Lesson Plans** suggest a study of David in the later book of the bible, a study of David's conquests and military prowess, viewing a filmstrip on David, a comparison of hero stories drawn from literature, and a discussion of the obstacles David overcame to become king of Israel.

The **Catechist Resource Sheet** contains a map of David's empire for use in class.

MODEL PRESENTATION

"The Voice of Practicality"

Topics to be presented:
1. Samuel and the Judges tell us of our need for independence.
2. David's life demonstrates our need for order.
3. Both independence and order are necessary in the mature person of faith.

Samuel

In the stories of the Judges and the great leader Samuel we learned an important truth about human nature—our tendency to forget our commitment and to become lazy. In these stories we saw how people had to be reawakened again and again from their sleepy acceptance of the *status quo*. We saw how people easily forgot God and even more easily slipped into the evil ways of the world around them. Samuel and the Judges kept telling Israel that its real strength lay in the willingness of each man and woman to care about God and their own freedom. They spent their lives calling Israel to personal responsibility and true freedom.

David

Today we will begin a study of another great leader of Israel, a man who emphasized a very different reality in Israel's life. This man was David. His contribution to Israel's life was his insistence on the need not for independence but for order. David sensed what every child already knows—that people need a family, a group which will accept them even when outsiders reject and hate them. David, as we shall see, built God's people into a great national family. That was David's role.

Most of us know something of the story of David from bible history classes. We have already heard how he was selected as Israel's second king after Saul, the first king, failed to obey the Lord. Most of us know the story of young David's battle with the giant Philistine, Goliath, and how he killed his enemy with a stone and a sling. We may have heard of David's friendship with Saul's son, Jonathan, his marriage to Saul's daughter, Michal, and his eventual succession to the throne of Israel after Saul's death. This outline of David's life is familiar enough to most teenagers.

What we can so easily overlook in all this, however, is David's passionate concern for the family of Israel. His only real interest throughout his younger years was the safety of his people—safety from foreign invaders like the Philistines and safety from intriguers like the witches who tricked Saul in his last days. For David, his people, his nation came first.

Once David had become king, he set about unifying his people, creating a sense of family among them. He built them a capitol where they could go to worship and to seek justice. This capitol was (and is) the city of Jerusalem. On top of a mountain David built a splendid city, one that made every Israelite proud of his heritage and always aware of the God who had given them such national glory.

David did more. He sent for the ancient ark of the covenant, the tent of worship from the desert days of Israel, the reminder that Israel was God's special people. When the ark was carried into Jerusalem, David led the people in a frenzied dance of welcome. David was so overjoyed that God and Israel were once more united that he forgot his kingly manners and jumped into the streets dancing and singing like a common peasant.

All through his middle years David fought battles with the enemies of Israel. He expanded Israel's borders in every direction and everywhere established peace. For the first time in generations, perhaps for the first time ever, Israel was able to enjoy the fruits of the Promised Land without an enemy to trouble them. All of this was David's contribution to building up the family of God's people.

Maturity

How can we admire both the fierce independence of Samuel and the Judges and the intense sense of nationhood of David? These two attitudes are poles apart. The Judges called upon people to be personally responsible for their lives. David called on them to submerge their personal desires into the desires of the national family. These attitudes of independence and interdependence are always in tension in our lives. It is this tension between these two ideals which keeps us balanced and leads us to maturity.

With our Church, for example, we must maintain some little distance from our leaders if we are to make their faith and vision of life really our own. Thus, we must always listen respectfully to what they say but jealously reserve to ourselves the right to make our own final decisions.

We must have a fierce loyalty to our Church and to its leaders. We must care about our fellow Church members.

The same may be said about our relationship with our nation. We must be at once independent and interdependent. We must be our own people and yet care intensely for all those others who are a part of our family.

Because we love our nation and our Church we will at times urge them on to greater holiness as Samuel and the Judges did. Because we love them we will even more often make great sacrifices for them as did David who so treasured the unity of God's own people.

PONDERING POINT

The Bishop's Role

In spite of all our sacralization, the bishop is a political leader. His task is to move his followers as best he can to some closer relationship with the Lord. Knowing the limits of his community, he must work always in the practical arena. He cannot afford the luxury of dabbling in the esoteric or chasing impossible ideals.

The political nature of the episcopacy is not often discussed. Liberals within the Church expect their bishops to be point men for change, great prophetic figures in the battle against mediocrity. Conservatives demand of their bishops that they turn back the clock and force all members of the Church into a mold made in olden days. Both demand from their bishops what they can never safely produce.

Bishops can only guide their communities where the communities wish to go. No amount of force, no amount of condemnation can force a community in a direction it does not yet appreciate. Nor, can any rules, regulations or denunciations keep a community from moving ahead when it is ready. At best, a good bishop can sense a community's highest ideals and lead toward fulfilling them.

A more realistic understanding of the political nature of the bishop's role in the Church will bring greater compassion for the men who are our leaders and shepherds in the faith.

PRIMARY LESSON PLAN

CLASS PLAN

Goal:
To show that living in community demands a cooperative stance.

Materials needed:
1) Copies, one per group of three, of the Task Sheet provided with this program. See page 107.
2) Pencils for each group
3) Blackboard, chalk and eraser
4) Newsprint, marking pen, masking tape
5) Bible

Methodology:
1. Using the Task Sheet, the students will experience working with the institutional church as a complement to the previous discussion of criticism in Lesson 5.
2. The catechist, using the material from the Model Presentation, "The Voice of Practicality," will present the contribution of David to the growth of Israel and at the same time show how cooperation complements criticism for those living in the community.

Opening prayer:
Psalm 23. An effective way to pray together is to read each verse and have the class respond: The Lord is my shepherd, I lack nothing.

Opening remarks:
In our last discussion we talked about the voices of criticism which are necessary if a community of freedom and law is not to degenerate into mere routine. Today, we will look at the other side of the coin—at cooperation with the community. Both attitudes are necessary in any community and, of course, in our church.

Task Sheet: *Allow about 15 minutes.*
Later today we will be talking about one of the really great people of the Old Testament—David, the king. But before we do, let's see how it feels to work in a cooperative situation within the church. Break into groups of three while I give you task sheets and pencils. Your task is to give the local parish council a little help. We will send your suggestions on to the parish council, possibly even arrange a meeting with them. *(Read directions.)* Any questions?

Reporting: *(Use newsprint or blackboard.)*
Now let's see what kind of ideas you came up with. I'll list your suggestions as we go along.

No. 1: What things can your parish do to meet the needs of young people of high school age? *(Call on groups in turn.)* Give us one of your answers and explain why you suggested it.

Repeat process for questions 2 and 3.

Those are very good suggestions. Please pass them to me now and we'll arrange to share these ideas with the parish council.

Discussion:
a) How did you feel about making suggestions to the parish council? Why?
b) Would you like to be a member of the parish council? Why? Why not?
c) What happens to groups that don't work together in making decisions?

SAVE POSTERS for the recap, Lesson 10.

Bridging:
It is so easy to become infatuated only with the voices of criticism in the church. They are, as we said before, important voices, voices we must listen to since they sometimes have the word of God. But, there are other voices, too, voices of cooperation. One of the greatest cooperators in the history of Israel was David . . .

Presentation:
Use the material from the Model Presentation, "The Voice of Practicality."

Discussion:
a) What impressed you most about David?
b) Why do all groups need people like David?
c) Do you think it is easier to be critical or cooperative with: the family, the church, the government, the school? Why?
d) Suppose you were asked to help the parish, would you accept?

Closing prayer:
(Psalm 8:1-6, 9. David praises the creator.)

Yahweh, our Lord,
how great your name throughout the earth!

Above the heavens is your majesty chanted
by the mouths of children, babes in arms.
You set your stronghold firm against your foes
to subdue enemies and rebels.

I look up at your heavens, made by your fingers,
at the moon and stars you set in place—
ah, what is man that you should spare a thought for him,
the son of man that you should care for him?

Yet you have made him little less than a god,
you have crowned him with glory and splendour,
made him lord over the work of your hands,
set all things under his feet.

Yahweh, our Lord,
how great your name throughout the earth!

Bible References

Chapter 13 of I Samuel begins the story of Saul's reign. The remaining chapters of I Samuel and all of II Samuel complete this story and relate David's rise to power. Sections of special interest are:

David and Goliath	I Samuel 17
David and Jonathan	I Samuel 18, 19, 20
David's Reaction to Saul's Death	II Samuel 1
David and the Ark	II Samuel 6

In Egypt, the Hebrews were grouped according to their fathers' houses and after the Exodus as the 12 tribes of Israel. The 12 sons of Jacob were:

Reuben

Simeon

Levi

Judah

Zebulun

Issachar

Dan

Gad

Asher

Naphtali

Joseph (Ephraim and Manasseh by later division)

Benjamin

ALTERNATE PLAN

CLASS PLAN

Goal:
To show that living in community demands a cooperative stance.

Materials needed:
1) List of suggestions compiled in the primary lesson. (See Task Sheet 6.) Or
2) Blackboard, chalk and eraser for formulating questions for parish council members
3) Bible
4) Permission slips, if required
5) If music is used, guitarist and words to the song, "I Have Made A Covenant"

Methodology:
1. The students will meet with representatives of their parish council and work with them to help the parish respond more fully to the needs of teenagers.
2. The catechist will lead a discussion of the merits of working with the system, of cooperating with those who direct institutional life and relate this to the life of David as described in the Model Presentation, "The Voice of Practicality."

Advance preparation:
This lesson plan builds on the primary lesson for this topic. The primary lesson plan asks the students to study the situation of teenagers in their parish and to make suggestions of ways the parish might better serve their needs. If the primary lesson is not used, some time will have to be spent with the students beforehand helping them focus on the needs of teens and list suggestions.

A second major preparation will be arranging a meeting with the parish council. The ideal meeting will take place at the regular parish council meeting, provided the council can set aside part of its time to dialogue with the students. Most councils will be interested in such a dialogue, even if only for the novelty of it.

If the parish council as a body cannot meet with the students, it may be possible to have a delegation of council members attend the regular class meeting for the dialogue.

The students should be prepared to make a presentation to the council members. One student might be delegated to show what the situation is locally vis-a-vis the teenagers and church, another to present teen needs and a third to present ways teenagers can cooperate with the council to help fill these needs. Also, ask one student to take notes during the discussion for use in the lesson No. 10 recap.

Opening prayer:
Read Ecclesiasticus 11:7-11, "Deliberation and Reflection."

Opening comments:
We are happy today to be able to work with the local leadership of our parish. Like us, they care what is happening to the teenagers of our area and want to help them. In a real way the parish council is for us what the leaders of Israel were to the

people of the Old Testament. Earlier we talked about the need for critical voices, like that of Samuel. Today we want to concentrate on cooperative voices, like that of David. Perhaps our dialogue with the parish council can help us understand in a practical way how important cooperation can be in getting the work of God accomplished.

Make introductions and allow time for the meeting.
(Press the students to ask questions of councilors and invite the councilors to question the students. The more open and honest the exchange the better for all concerned.)

Catechist's presentation:

At this time the catechist, in the presence of the councilors if possible, may wish to review the Model Presentation, "The Voice of Practicality," or, if the class has not done the primary lesson, present the material for the first time.

Discussion:

Now that we have had the experience of working with a parish council, let's talk a little about it.

1. How did you feel during the discussion? Did you feel important, helpful, respected? Why?
2. Do you think the councilors felt comfortable talking with you? Why? Why not?
3. Can you see how this kind of cooperation is helpful for all concerned? Why? Why not?
4. Do you think David met and talked with his people? Why?
5. Suppose Samuel had been sitting here during the meeting, how do you think he would have reacted? Would this have been helpful? Why? Why not?

Closing prayer: (Psalm 89:1-2, 3-4, 20-21, 24 and 26.)

If possible, sing together "I Have Made A Covenant" with musical accompaniment. Otherwise, pray together the following responsorial psalm:

Response: For ever I will sing the goodness of the Lord.

I will celebrate your love for ever, Lord,
age after age my words shall proclaim your
    faithfulness;
for I claim that love is built to last for ever
and your faithfulness founded firmly in the
    heavens.   R. For ever . . .

"I have made a covenant with my Chosen,
I have given my servant David my sworn word:
I have founded your dynasty to last for ever,
I have built you a throne to outlast all time.   R. For ever . . .

I have selected my servant David
and anointed him with my holy oil;
my hand will be constantly with him,
he will be able to rely on my arm.   R. For ever . . .

With my faithfulness and love,
his fortunes shall rise in my name.
He will invoke me, "My father,
my God and rock of my safety."   R. For ever . . .

MINI LESSON PLANS

The purpose of the ideas which follow is to provide the creative teacher with further suggestions for classroom experiences related to the original Model Presentation.

Bible Research

This is a helpful way of understanding the impact of David on later Hebrew and Christian thought. With the aid of a concordance available in most Catholic and in all public libraries, look up the name David and trace the many times it is used in later Old Testament and in New Testament books. This can be a class project. Xerox the references to David and then cut them up into several sections, one for each group of three students. Ask each group of students to report to the whole class giving such information as: (1) What does David seem to symbolize in later writings? (2) Are the later references true to the story of David as recorded in 2 Samuel? (3) Why was David seen as a hero? (4) Who in present life situations would be similar to David? Other questions will easily prolong the class and add zest to it.

David the Conqueror

David's conquests are easily appreciated from the map on page 108. A discussion on this aspect of David's life will result from the following and similar questions: (1) Do you think Samuel's warning about kings was justified in David's lifetime? (2) Do you know other warriors who are heroes? saints? (3) Is war a holy act if carried out against unbelievers? Communists? (4) Can a Christian believer be a pacifist?

Filmstrip Study

Studying people of this century who were leaders like David is possible using two of the components of *Images of the New Man*, Thomas S. Klise Co., Box 3418, Peoria, Illinois 61614. The appropriate sections are "John Kennedy" and "Pope John."

David and Goliath

This is the most famous of the David stories. In it the weak and powerless underdog overcomes the powerful conqueror. A similar story is the fable of the tortoise and the hare. Ask students to list all the similar stories from literature and from real life which they can think of. In a discussion, help the students to discover the universal appeal for such stories and the reasons for that appeal.

David the Valiant

A study of David's life as recorded in 2 Samuel will reveal a long list of obstacles he met and overcame. Ask students in groups to list as many as they can discover. Then, discuss other great men and women who met and mastered obstacles. Ask why some seem able to persever in the face of trouble and others so easily give up.

TASK SHEET 6

Cooperation

Many young Catholics have little contact with their parishes. They may go to Mass on Sunday but, other than Mass and CCD class, spend little time there.

Let's suppose your group is asked to help your parish council minister to the needs of the youth in your parish. Answer the following questions and, if possible, share your findings with your real parish council.

1. What things can your parish (parishes) do to meet the needs of young people of high school age?

    A _____
    B _____
    C _____
    D _____

2. What things could the parish council invite youth to do to meet the needs of others in the parish?

    A _____
    B _____
    C _____
    D _____

3. What changes in the way the parish operates would be helpful in ministering to the needs of young people?

    A _____
    B _____
    C _____
    D _____
    _____
    _____
    _____

(Duplicator master of this sheet in packet)

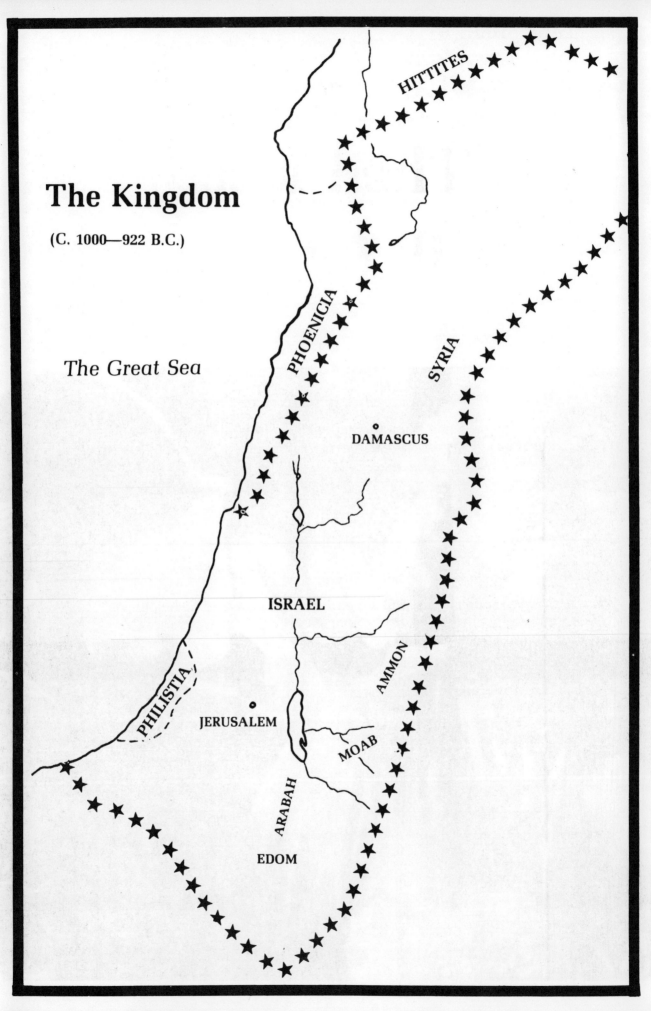

7
The Price of Faith

CATECHIST'S BACKGROUND

Community

This generation of Catholics has sought an elusive ideal—community. Since Vatican II, Catholic people have alternately hoped and despaired of finding the unity of faith spelled out in a concrete group of here and now people. All of our theology has been recast in terms of community. The Church has been proclaimed a community. The sacraments have been explained as signs of that community. Faith has been seen as the entry point into the community. Moral demands are demands which arise from the community's sense of its own destiny and its realization of the presence of Jesus within it.

Yet, with nearly two decades of search for community, few Catholics feel they have discovered it. In the later life of the great king, David, may be one of the most profound lessons one can learn about this quest.

Faith brings with it freedom. Freedom in its turn demands both community and law. To live in this community spawned by faith one must possess both the independence of Samuel and the Judges and the commitment to community of David. Yet, such dedication and commitment to the community has its price, a price which clearly demonstrates the tragedy of all community life.

For community to grow its members must open up their lives to one another. All must risk their sensibilities by revealing more and more about themselves. Each person must grow to care about the other members of the community. All must grow into a kind of family relationship. Once this happens each member who has loved the others becomes vulnerable to those he or she has loved. In time, it is nearly always the case that someone will misunderstand and reach out to hurt.

Even in the most intense community, then, there is some hurt and some loneliness. Because community is not God, it can never fulfill all human desires. This simple fact of religious life, is one which has been largely overlooked in the past 20 years in Catholic circles.

David's family

There are few stories more marked with tragedy than David's love for his family. The Second Book of Samuel recounts the intricate struggles of David's sons to seize power from him. Here we learn of Amnon's rape of his half sister, Tamar, his subsequent murder by Absalom and finally the rebellion against David which Absalom, David's own son, led.

In all these stories the theme of betrayal reoccurs again and again. David, the loving father, the indulgent parent, was betrayed by those whom he most loved, by his own flesh and blood. His intense desire for family unity and religious community was betrayed by the sons to whom he gave so much.

Sheba's revolt

David's second great attempt to build community was among his own people. Even here he experienced treachery. In the later years of David's life, a man of the tribe of Ben-

David was known as the Lion of Judah.

jamin, Judah's most trusted ally, launched a second rebellion. David called this rebellion more dangerous than Absalom's attempted coup had ever been. The Benjaminite's name was Sheba. To his cause flocked the majority of the ten Northern tribes. The old alliance on which Israel's nationhood and David's community rested was broken. Only determined armed force was able to preserve the union. In the end the rebellion was crushed and Sheba killed but the message to David was clear. Only through force and power was he able to control the nation he had fashioned. In the end, his desire for community was never fulfilled.

From this lesson of David today's Catholics can learn the truth about community. Community is always elusive, always difficult to attain and even once attained requires great discipline and even force to keep it from fragmenting and destroying itself. Christian community is not unlike this community experience of David. However one may dream of a community without rules and without some force, it is difficult to maintain cohesion without these seemingly alien elements.

David the man

David was a forceful and determined young man, one who overcame all obstacles to achieve his goal. Once accepted as king, David's character seems to have mellowed. His concerns seem less for power and more for his own personal development. II Samuel tells the touching story of David's adulterous relationship with Bethsheba. This young woman caught the king's eye early in his career. Her husband was fighting in one of David's petty wars. In the absence of her husband, Bethsheba had relations with David and conceived a child.

If Bethsheba were found with child while her husband was in battle she would have been stoned to death as an adulteress. David recalled her husband, Uriah, from the field. He returned reluctantly but refused to live with his wife, so great was his military zeal. Faced with Uriah's refusal to go to Bethsheba, David arranged for the loyal soldier to die in battle, thus saving Bethsheba's honor and providing David with another wife.

The prophet Nathan called David to repentance. Quickly and with unaffected passion David returned to the Lord. As a result of his sin, the baby born of this union died, we are told, and David himself felt the full force of his sorrow and guilt. An ancient tradition tells us that he wrote the Fifty-First Psalm during this period of grief.

David's inability to discipline his own sons has already been noted. He failed to punish Amnon for his rape of Tamar and later failed to curb young Absalom's ambition. Both failures resulted in tragedy for the sons and for David.

What emerges from the stories in The Second Book of Samuel is the picture of a middle-aged monarch who had lost the resoluteness of his earlier years. He had slowly given in to the luxury of the life of his court, discovered the infidelity of his own children and came to depend almost completely on a cadre of professional soldiers to maintain order in his kingdom. What must have seemed a lofty goal in young David's life became the setting for a series of personal tragedies and left David a tired and disspirited old man, unsure of his own family and unaware of many of the intrigues which moved about him in his final days.

Pedagogy

The purpose of this lesson is to illustrate the difficulties of living with the community of faith and to help students to form realistic expectations of their relationship with the Church. The **Primary Lesson Plan** begins with a discussion of the problems which come with being special. The **Model Presentation** shows how David's special character of faith and success brought him the misunderstanding of the envious. The **Alternate Lesson Plan** suggests a role play which involves the characters mentioned in the section of II Samuel covered in this lesson.

The **Mini Lesson Plans** suggest a study of David's relationships with several characters in II Samuel, a reading of some of the psalms, a simulation of the Absalom-David campaign, a study of the symbolic nature of David, and a research assignment about Solomon's Temple.

The **Catechist Resource Sheet** contains a list of the principal characters in David's later life with a description of each.

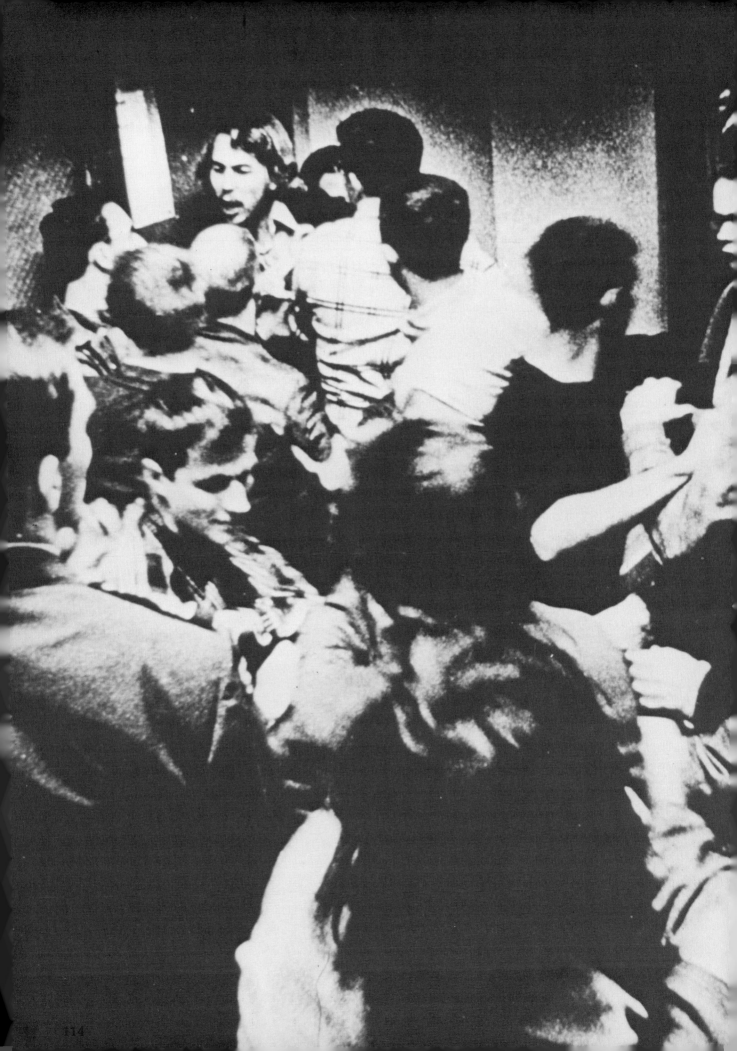

MODEL PRESENTATION

"The Price of Faith"

Topics to be presented:

1. David's own family and his own people misunderstood and disappointed him.
2. Misunderstanding and loneliness often accompany faith even in the best of communities.
3. Realistic expectations of our faith communities will help us avoid bitter disappointment with them.

David's family

Like all potentates of his day, David had many wives. Because he did, he set the stage for internal rivalry among his wives and children. The Second Book of Samuel records some of these intense struggles and their effect upon David. So vivid are these stories that many scholars believe they were written by an eyewitness or even by a member of the court who was actually involved in them.

David's oldest son and next in line to the throne was Amnon. Amnon inherited some of his father's violence and penchant for direct action. One day he noticed that he was attracted to his half sister, Tamar. David's own nephew encouraged the young Amnon to trap the girl in his bedroom and later to rape her. After this rape, Amnon grew to hate Tamar and refused to see her or help her in any way.

With his characteristic indulgence for his sons, David refused to punish Amnon for what he had done. Tamar's full brother, Absalom also David's son, took the law into his own hands and brutally murdered Amnon. He then fled the kingdom and lived as an exile. David was heartbroken.

After mourning Amnon's death, David relented of his anger toward Absalom and allowed him to return to Jerusalem. Once returned Absalom quietly built up a personal following and plotted to murder David. With the help of some of David's most trusted advisors, Absalom proclaimed himself king and drove David into exile. Only David's professional bodyguards remained loyal to him. It seemed that David's own family, his most trusted counselors and the whole nation he had served so well cared little about their former king.

In the subsequent battle between the forces of Absalom and the soldiers loyal to David, Absalom was killed. Once more David was stricken with grief. In returning to Jerusalem and to his kingship David found little joy. Now two of his sons were dead and he an old man who seemed to be loved neither by his family nor by his own people about whom he cared so deeply.

Alienation and Loneliness

David's faith and love of the community brought him to great maturity. He learned both his need for independence and his need to depend on others, especially his general, Joab, and his army. Yet, this maturity was not accompanied by great joy. Faith led David to sadness, great sadness at times.

The very fact that he cared so deeply for others made him all the more vulnerable to their attacks. Because David loved his own sons so much, they were able to hurt him more than did any other people.

In David's life we learn something of the paradox of living in the community or family of faith. We enter that community to share strength with others who have had the same experience of God as we. Indeed, such comfort and such strength are in our communities but so, too, are misunderstanding, loneliness and alienation. Even the best of communities, even our own families, can never completely fill our longing for brotherhood. This final loneliness can be cured only by an intimate friendship with the Lord.

David discovered this truth about faith and faith community in Absalom's rebellion. Jesus discovered it in his betrayal by Judas. Even before this, Jesus warned his disciples that their enemies would spring out of their own families and it was fellow family members who would turn them over to the government for persecution. Even in Jesus' own lifetime, faith and the community which followed it still brought with it a certain loneliness, misunderstanding, and even alienation.

Realistic expectations

What was true for David and later for Jesus is true today. No believer can expect from the Church, the parish, the neighborhood, or any other group of people complete acceptance and complete security. That kind of acceptance and security comes only from the Lord. Moreover, it is possible that one's greatest disappointments will come not from outsiders but from members of one's own group. Those to whom we open our hearts are the people who have the greatest power to harm us.

Faced with this reality of life, some will become cynics and leave the community to go it alone. They will fear having friends and always hold back in their relationships with others. More mature people, however, will go beyond this cynicism and take from the community the strength it has to offer but never expect from it what no human group can ever provide. The true believer will understand that he or she can never place his complete trust in any group, however holy it may be. Complete trust and total faith can be given to God alone.

Only the Lord is trustworthy enough to receive the complete gift of self we call faith. This was the meaning of the first of Moses' commandments. It is also the message of David's dealings with his own family. It is what we learn from Jesus' life. In a nutshell it is, "Community is good but only God is worthy of faith."

PONDERING POINT

Isolation Within Community

Community, we are told by both sociologists and theologians, will be the answer to all our modern problems. Sociologists tell us that when neighborhoods are reestablished family life will improve. Theologians tell us that only community building can save the modern parish. In a sense, these scholars are correct, In another sense, their ideas are misleading.

Saint Augustine's famous quotation, "Our hearts are restless until they rest in Thee," is as true today as it has always been. Community is not God. It cannot take away all our inner searching nor all our loneliness.

Saint Francis of Assisi, the man who founded the great community of Franciscans, died with but a few friends to support him. The community he had founded looked upon him with respect but could not find for him the place of leadership he deserved. Jesus, himself, formed community with his disciples but died on the cross with only a few comforters. Community in both cases was able to provide only some of the needs of these great people and, in the end, was itself a disappointment.

To say all this is not to deny the need for community but only to caution against unreal expectations. Community is the work of humankind. Like all the works of our hands it is flawed and imperfect. Only the Lord can fill all our human needs. Only He is without flaw, only He, perfect.

PRIMARY LESSON PLAN

CLASS PLAN

Goal:
To show how faith usually brings with it some isolation.

Materials needed:
1) Copies, one per group of three, of the Task Sheet provided with this program, See page 123.
2) Blank paper, pencil for each student
3) Blackboard, chalk and eraser
4) Newsprint, marking pen, masking tape
5) Bible

Methodology:
1. Using the Task Sheet, the students will imagine what happens to a mythical character who knows some important secret.
2. The catechist, using the material from the Model Presentation, "The Price of Faith," will recount the story of David and Absalom and point out that faith brings a certain loneliness and misunderstanding.

Opening prayer: (Psalm 51:1-4, 8-13)

David, the great man of faith and leader of Israel, was to taste the bitterness of sin. The prophet Nathan condemned David's relationship with Bathsheba and called on him to repent. In the following psalm, David expresses to God his deep sorrow for his sin.

Have mercy on me, O God, in your goodness,
in your great tenderness wipe away my faults;
wash me clean of my guilt,
purify me from my sin.

For I am well aware of my faults,
I have my sin constantly in mind,
having sinned against none other than you,
having done what you regard as wrong.

Instill some joy and gladness into me,
let the bones you have crushed rejoice again.
Hide your face from my sins,
wipe out all my guilt.

God, create a clean heart in me,
put into me a new and constant spirit,
do not banish me from your presence,
do not deprive me of your holy spirit.

Be my saviour again, renew my joy,
keep my spirit steady and willing;
and I shall teach transgressors the way to you,
and to you the sinners will return.

Opening remarks:

For several weeks now we have been talking about the kind of attitude one must have to live in faith within the community founded on freedom and law. Remember how we talked about the necessity of a critical attitude and then a cooperative one, as well. So many think that if they are cooperative, the community, and all in that community, will like them and make their lives happy for them. This is unfortunately not the case, as we shall see in the story of David and his son, Absalom.

Task sheet: *Allow about 15 minutes.*

Before we talk about David and Absalom, let's look at a rather humorous task sheet. *(Pass out sheets and pencils.)* It asks you to imagine you are watching a television program and your set breaks down in the middle of the story. You then go to bed and imagine your own ending. Any questions?

Reporting:

I'm anxious to hear how the story ends! *(Write brief description of each group's ending on newsprint or the blackboard.)*

Listen closely to the endings and, after all groups have reported, we'll choose the one we think is best. *(Call on all groups.)*

Discussion: SAVE POSTERS for the recap, Lesson 10.

a) Which ending did you like best? A show of hands for group 1's story—group 2's story, etc.
b) Why did you particularly like that ending?
c) How do you think most people reacted to June? Why?

Bridging:

June, the girl in our story, finds herself more and more isolated because she knows something not everyone knows. Even though she is trying to help her city, they do not really care much about her and her feelings. That is about the way it was with David in the later years of his reign as king. He had organized the kingdom, brought peace to the land and ruined all the enemies of the Jews. But, the people soon forgot his many good deeds and found they did not really like him as they had in earlier days. Before we talk about David, take out paper and pencil and write: "If I had been David I would have . . ." We'll share your answers after my short presentation.

Presentation:

Use the material from the Model Presentation, "The Price of Faith."

Discussion:

a) Who will volunteer to share his or her reflection statement, "If I had been David I would have . . ." (Call on volunteers and invite comments.)
b) Does June on today's task sheet remind you of David? In what ways?
c) Does David remind you of Jesus? Why?
d) What is the best way to handle the loneliness caused by the misunderstanding and/or jealousy of others?

Closing prayer: (Psalm 3:1-6)

This prayer of David reveals his feelings as he is escaping from his son Absalom.

Bible References

The story of Absalom is recorded in II Samuel 13-19, a relatively short section. Other passages of interest which occurred during David's reign are:

The Story of Bathsheba — II Samuel 11 and 12

The Revolt of Sheba — II Samuel 20

David's Census — II Samuel 24

ALTERNATE PLAN

CLASS PLAN

Goal:
To show how faith usually brings with it some isolation.

Materials needed:
1) Bibles for role play preparation and prayers
2) Pencil and paper for each student
3) If music is used, guitarist and words to "Hear O Lord."

Methodology:
1. The students will role play a courtroom scene in which Absalom is on trial for his rebellion against David. The defense attorney will attack David's character and reign as king in his defense of Absalom.
2. The catechist will lead a discussion of this experience and tie it into the material from the Model Presentation, "The Price of Faith."

Advance preparation:
At least a week before the class, the catechist will appoint various class members to play the following roles:

David	Prosecuting attorney
Absalom	Defense attorney
Amon	Shimei
Thamar	Zadok
Joab	Hushai
Judge	The Jury

The entire story of the revolt is contained in 2 Samuel, chapters 13 through 19. Of course, it will be necessary to imagine Absalom was not killed by Joab but captured.

Tell the two attorneys (the key characters in such a role play) that they may infer as much as they wish from the text, but can also use the text to check each other's accuracy.

Opening prayer:
Lord, I understand the loneliness of David.
    I, too, know what it is to be without friends
        and to face life with all its contradictions by myself.
    Let me have the courage David had.
    And, let me come to understand that you are friend
        enough
            even in this troubled land of ours. Amen.

Opening comments:
Today we will be role playing one of the most tragic of all the Bible stories—the revolt of Absalom against his father, David. The story is tragic because there was some reason for Absalom's revolt and tragic because David seems to have been well meaning and sincere in spite of his shortcomings. Perhaps we can see in David the loneliness that comes to all persons of faith. But, more of that later.

Role play:
Now we will begin our courtroom scene. Does everyone understand his role? Please, then, take your places—the judge at the bench, Absalom and his attorney to the judge's right and the prosecutor to the judge's left. All witness remain in your regular

seats until you are called to testify. The jury should sit to the left of the judge. Ready? Let's begin. *Allow about 30 minutes.*

What is the verdict of the jury? *(Allow time for deliberation.)* I found our trial very interesting. Thank you.

Discussion:

Now that we have seen our courtroom scene come to its conclusion, let's talk a little about what happened in the lives of David and Absalom.

1. If you were in David's place, how would you have felt when you received word that Absalom was in revolt?
2. How did David's faith experience make him different from people around him?
3. David seemed to forgive Amon, but Absalom could not. Why was this?
4. Do you know anyone alive today who possesses David's spirit of forgiveness and faith? Please tell us about this person.
5. Do you know anyone alive today who has Absalom's sense of vengeance? Please tell us about this person.

Catechist's presentation:

Here, the catechist may wish to review the Model Presentation, "The Price of Faith," or, if the class has not done the primary lesson, present the material for the first time. An introduction to a first time presentation:

We have seen how the lives of David and Absalom were tragically intertwined. Behind all David's mistakes and weaknesses lies something great, his faith. That faith led David into a lonely life.

Reflections: *(Give students pencils and paper.)*

a) What impressed me most about David was . . .
b) While you were talking I wondered about . . .
c) If I had been David I would have . . .
d) When I am lonely, I . . .

Closing prayer:

If possible, sing together "Hear O Lord" together with musical accompaniment. Otherwise, read the words and follow with a period of quiet reflection.

Hear O Lord, the sound of my
    call,
Hear O Lord and have mercy.
My soul is longing for the glory
    of you,
Hear O Lord and answer me.

Every night before I sleep,
I pray my soul to take.
Or else I pray that loneliness
Is gone when I awake.

Hear O Lord, the sound of my
    call,
Hear O Lord and have mercy.
My soul is longing for the glory
    of you,
Hear O Lord and answer me.

MINI LESSON PLANS

The purpose of the ideas which follow is to provide the creative teacher with further suggestions for classroom experiences related to the original Model Presentation.

Relationships With Others

These are the true tests of a person's character. Fortunately, we have considerable information about David's relationships with several of his contemporaries. A good lesson would be to examine these relationships. Assign each group one of the following people: Samuel, Saul, Jonathan, Michal, Abner, Joab, Bathsheba, and Uriah. Ask each group to study the relationship of David with the character they have been assigned. After a half hour invite each group to report to the class. From the several relationships the central characterisitcs of David, the man, will begin to emerge.

The Psalms

The Psalms are the great prayers of David or so many of them are reputed. An interesting project is either to rewrite one of the psalms using images similar to the original but ones known and understood in our contemporary culture, or to write original psalms using the form of one of the psalms.

Absalom or David

Absalom for king or David for king must have been the cries of Jerusalem during the days of Absalom's rebellion. Ask the class to prepare an election campaign for the two men complete with slogans, reasons for the superiority of the one over the other, posters, etc. At the end of the class have each group put on its campaign for the other. If possible, invite in neutral people, (another class or a group of parents) to decide how they would vote or even actually to vote by secret ballot.

David as model of Jesus

Many ancient writers saw remarkable similarities between the life of David and that of Jesus. Jesus is called "son of David" in the New Testament. Ask the students, either for a group assignment or as a class discussion, to identify as many points of similarity between the two men as possible. The following are a few hints: 1) both were kings; 2) both were betrayed by their close followers; 3) both died in Jerusalem; 4) both died before their work seemed to be finished.

Solomon's Temple

The Temple of Solomon was built about this time—in the generation after David's death. Ask students to research the Temple, its decorations and the sacrifices offered there. This will give the class some of the flavor of the times of David and his court. It will also show them the opulence against which the life of David was set and how difficult it must have been for the man to remain a good person.

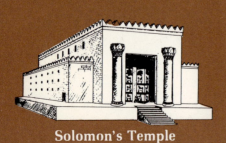
Solomon's Temple

TASK SHEET 7

Writing Your Own Ending

You are watching a television movie when your television set breaks. You go to bed and before you fall asleep you try to imagine how the story might have ended. Read the first part of the story and then write your own ending.

June is a delightful young woman, pretty, vivacious, popular. Everybody loves her, her parents, her friends at school and her many boyfriends, too.

One night June is awakened from sleep by a strange, hissing sound in the corner of her room. As she shakes the sleep from her eyes, she thinks she sees a tall man standing in the corner and a soft light is shining from his intense eyes. Strangely, she is not afraid.

For a long time the strange visitor does not speak. June just sits in bed looking at him and feeling very happy in his presence.

Finally, the strange man speaks. "June," he says, "are you afraid?"

"No," she answers truthfully.

"Good," the strange man replies. "I want you to know a very important secret. In six months, a hydrogen bomb stored in the arsenal at the edge of town will explode. Because you are so popular and so well liked by everyone, I hope you can talk the people in the town into leaving before that date."

"But, me? How can I? I am just a teenager."

"No matter your age. Just do your best."

The next morning June talked it over with her parents and CRACKLE—POP—STOP

Your ending:_____

_____
_____
_____
_____
_____
_____
_____
_____
_____
_____

(Duplicator master of this sheet in packet)

CATECHIST RESOURCE SHEET

The Principal Characters of the David Story

Samuel, the acknowledged religious and political leader of all the tribes of Israel in the last generation before Israel united to form a nation. It was he who advised against a strong central government and the institution of the monarchy but who gave in to the popular demand for a king and appointed first Saul and later David. He seems to have been a strong supporter of David during his last days.

Saul, the first king of Israel, was deposed by Samuel and later killed in a battle with the Philistines. He was the father of David's best friend, Jonathan, and one of David's wives, Michal. Saul first loved David and enjoyed his services as a musician and later a warrior. Later he turned against David and sought to kill him. David never turned completely against Saul and spared his life on at least two occasions.

Jonathan was Saul's son and David's closest friend. He saved David from his father's wrath and helped him escape from a palace intrigue. Jonathan was killed while fighting with his father, Saul.

Michal was a daughter of Saul and David's wife. She seems to have been a proud young woman. She scoffed at David for dancing before the ark of the Lord during its introduction into Jerusalem. David rejected her and turned to other wives.

Joab was David's cousin and the commander of his troops. He seems to have been a very strong willed and somewhat devious man, one of whom David disapproved but was unable to punish. Joab killed Abner, the leader of the Northern tribes, Absalom, David's son, Amasa, one of David's generals and Uriah, the husband of Bathsheba. Before he died David asked his son, Solomon, to execute Joab after his own death and so punish the evils of his lifetime which David had been unwilling or unable to do.

Abner was a commander of Saul's forces. After Saul's death he rallied ten of the twelve tribes to Ishbaal, Saul's son, and set up a kingdom, Mahanaim. During the war which followed between the followers of David and those of Ishbaal he remained faithful to Saul's line. When his troops were defeated he tried to lead the ten tribes into David's camp. Just as he was to deliver them to David, Joab killed him. David rejected this killing and praised Abner's life and devotion to the family of Saul.

Bathsheba was the wife of Uriah, a professional soldier in David's army. David seduced her and sent her husband into an impossible battle situation so that he would be killed. Her first son by David died as a punishment for their sin. Her second son, Solomon, became the successor of David.

Solomon was David's son and his chosen successor as king. Little is known of his relationship with his father.

8 Prophecy

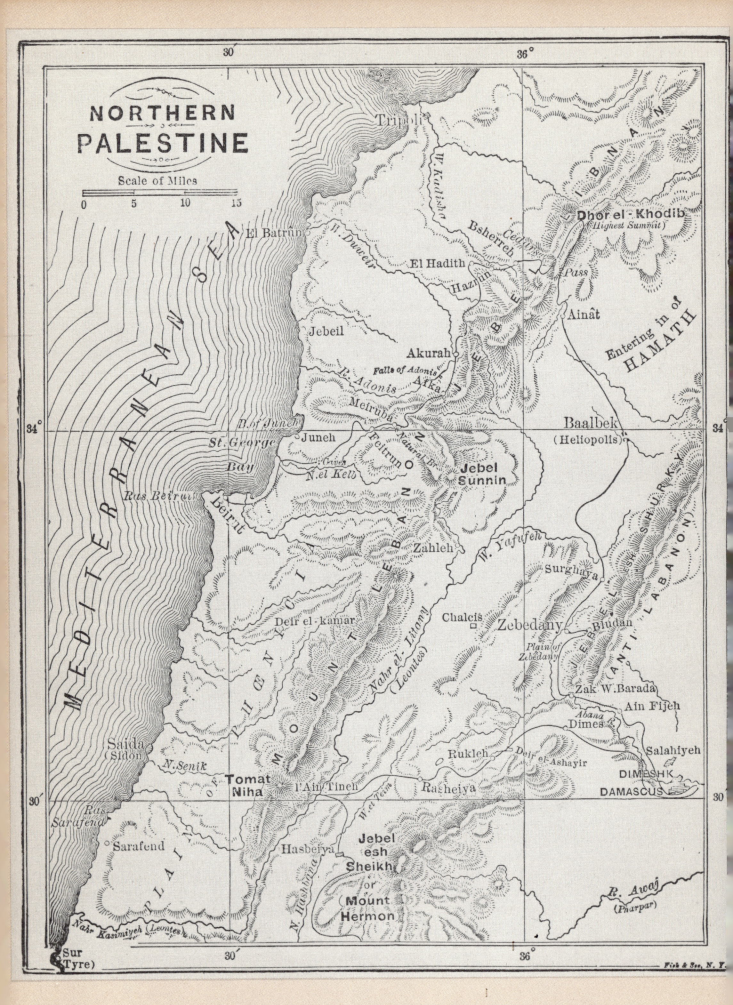

CATECHIST'S BACKGROUND

Historical setting

David assumed leadership in Israel about 1000 B.C. He died in 961. Upon his death, the rule of the 12 tribes passed to his son, Solomon. Solomon's reign was a time of peace and national prosperity. It was also a time for great public building projects, the most glorious of which was the Jerusalem Temple, one of the wonders of the ancient world. The price of such grandiose building efforts was an intensification of the unrest among the nobles and the common people whose forced labor and possessions provided the raw material for these projects.

In 922 B.C. Solomon died. He was succeeded by his brash and spoiled son, Rehoboam. Before his coronation, the spokesmen of the Northern tribes begged Rehoboam to change the policies which had made his father's rule so onerous. When he refused, the 10 Northern tribes withdrew from the monarchy and under Jeroboam I set up a kingdom of their own at Samaria in Northern Palestine. From that point on, the 12 tribes were never again united under a single ruler.

The Northern kingdom was faced with a difficult religious and political problem. David had centered all worship of Yahweh in Jerusalem. There Solomon had built a temple to the Lord and established the official worship ceremonial. To enter Jerusalem was to leave the Northern kingdom and to seem to show some disloyalty to the court at Samaria. Faced with this dilemma, Jeroboam I set up shrines of his own in the North. These shrines never enjoyed the legitimacy of Jerusalem and often lapsed into pagan rituals.

The Northern kingdom existed for 200 years. In 721 B.C. the armies of Sargon, king of Assyria conquered Samaria. The people were deported to Assyria where they were assimilated into the population. This experience of conquest and assimilation is often referred to by the expression "the 10 lost tribes of Israel."

The Southern kingdom fared somewhat better. With its capital at Jerusalem it continued in existence until about 587 B.C. when its last king, Zedekiah, and the ruling families were taken into exile by the Babylonians. In 539 B.C. the people of Judah were allowed to return to Jerusalem and rebuild their city. Through a stormy history this new kingdom usually ruled not by kings but by the priestly caste endured until 70 A.D. when the city was completely destroyed by the Roman general Titus.

The prophetic movement

The identification of religious and civil power under the kings in both the Northern and the Southern kingdoms brought with it a tendency toward mediocrity. Religious leaders too easily supported the whims of the kings and court and themselves became puppets of the ruling class. With no special mission other than pleasing the king, priests often prostituted the worship of the one God with rites drawn from the fertility cults of the native peoples who had never been totally assimilated.

Had there been no independent voice raised in both kingdoms the worship of Yahweh might well have been quietly forgotten or transformed into just another of the many fertility rites. As a matter of fact, however, strong voices did arise to call the rulers and the ordinary people back to the first fervor of their covenant relationship with the Lord. These strong voices were the prophets, a religious movement unique, it seems, in Israel.

The prophet often had no connection with the official religious leadership of the time. He was a lay person who experienced God in some intensely personal way and felt compelled to deliver God's message to all who would listen. He was not one who foretold the future as such (a popular misconception) but one who delivered the call of God to repentance and incidentally warned of the dire consequences which would befall the people who did not heed God's call.

Elijah

Elijah was an early prophet and in many ways the father of prophecy. Elijah confronted the court of the Northern kingdom at a time when it was particularly corrupt. The king, Ahab, and his legendary wife, Jezebel, lived in great luxury, worshipped pagan gods and practiced brutal injustice upon the people. Elijah promised a great drought as a punishment. The drought lasted three years. Finally, in a contest with the priests of the pagan god, Baal, Elijah dramatically broke the drought. In spite of his pleas, however, the kingdom did not undergo any great religious revival until after his death.

After Elijah, Elisha took over the prophet's mantle. Associated with him was a "family of prophets," a kind of counter-cultural group, who kept alive the purity of the old desert covenant. This group, scholars believe, wrote the second of the important sources for the Book of Genesis. During this period the center of Israelite reform and religious life was located not in the Jerusalem Temple but with the group of poor and itinerant prophets organized by Elisha.

For centuries prophetic voices were raised in both kingdoms. We know little of some of these inspired men, not even their names. Of others, we have permanent written records. Amos, Micah and Hosea all prophesied about 750 B.C., a time when the Northern kingdom was about to go into exile. The words of Amos still startle the sensibilities of the refined. Hosea, on the other hand, was a cultured court official who spoke to the people in mystical allegories. The style of prophecy seemed to follow the individual prophet's social standing and education but the message was always the same, a call to return to the fervor of the desert covenant and there to rediscover faith, community, and the rule of God's law.

A final flurry of prophecy took place about the time the Southern kingdom was to enter its Babylonian captivity. The great prophets Isaiah, Jeremiah, and Ezekiel all prepared the people for their ordeal and saw them through the two generations of exile. Later editors have undoubtedly added many passages to these books of prophecy, but again the outline of their message was the same clear call to return to the first fervor of Israel's desert life.

Summing up the prophetic movement is not easy. Each of the prophets presents a fascinating character study. The writings of the prophets which remain to us are filled with mystical allusion and allegory. Yet, the very fact that such a line of men without any official or institutional blessing continued to rise to challenge the spirit of the times is the reason for the preservation of monotheism and covenant among the Hebrew people. While their monarchy and Temple worship fell into disrepute, the prophets maintained the ideal and in the longrun built the faith of the people Israel.

Pedagogy

This lesson attempts to stress the importance of the prophetic voice in Israel and in our own day. The **Primary Lesson Plan** asks students to search for prophets at work in their own environment. The **Model Presentation** recounts the setting for prophecy and tells the story of Elijah. The **Alternate Lesson Plan** presents a bible search which shows the influence of the prophets on the life and times of Jesus.

The **Mini Lesson Plans** present several suggestions for filmstrip study, a role playing incident based on the life of Elijah, a discussion of contemporary prophets, and a short research task.

The **Catechist Resource Sheet** contains an explanation of the function of the prophet and sketches of the most prominent prophets.

MODEL PRESENTATION
"Prophecy"

Topics to be presented:
1. As Israel grew prosperous and secure, it lost its interest in the covenant.
2. Elijah and the other prophets recalled Israel to the covenant commitment.
3. Prophets in today's world call us to our highest Christian ideals.

National complacency

Sometimes it is less trouble to build a fire than to keep it blazing day after day. It is easier to plant a garden than to keep it weeded all summer long. This is the way it was with Israel. With David, Israel's nationhood became an accomplished fact. What began as a tiny seed of faith in the hearts of a few brave and different men like Abraham and Moses was now a political reality. But, how rekindle that tiny flame of faith in generations who grew up with the nation as a taken-for-granted fact of life? Without personal faith and a personal response the nation of Israel would be no more than a hollow shell of memory, lacking all personal vitality in its members.

God's answer to this human problem of rekindling personal faith and the personal awareness of freedom, community, and law was to send His messengers—the prophets. These were men who were known, not as predictors of the future but as men who spoke about the present. These were strong men in the tradition of Samuel and the Judges who saw injustice and evil in the life of the nation and called people to repentance.

During the 400 years between the time of David and the exile of the Jewish people in Babylon (1000 B.C.—597 B.C.), there were many of these messengers. How many we do not know. The bible speaks of some of them and alludes to the existence of many more. What these men had in common was not a new theology nor a breakthrough in the thought patterns of their people, but a simple, practical call to live the life of the nation's dreams and highest aspirations.

Elijah

The earliest prophet of whom we have extensive records was Elijah. In the days of Elijah the Northern Kingdom with its capital at Samaria had fallen into the most offensive immorality. Stories of the selfishness, the greed, and the loss of a consciousness of the nation's ideals abound in the bible. The king at the time, Ahab, murdered one of his subjects in order to take possession of his farm. The king's wife, Jezebel, led many of the court people to outlandish rites of fertility worship. All in all, the kingdom of Israel was losing its grasp on the reason for its existence as it forgot both its God and its sense of brotherhood.

Into this scene came Elijah, something of a fierce and unlettered man himself. He proclaimed that the Lord would send drought upon the land. And drought there was, three years without rain. At the end of that time, Elijah dramatically appeared to challenge the priests of the pagan god Baal to send rain. When they failed after a long day of prayers, sacrifices, and personal pain, Elijah dramatically mounted the stage and prayed to the Lord of Heaven. Rain came. It came in buckets. So great was it that the priests of Baal were destroyed in the process. Israel turned back to the Lord for a time and rekindled the fervor of its faith.

Elijah's life was marked by many strange happenings and by great achievements. He anointed Elisha his successor as prophet to Israel, appointed Jehu a new king of the people, foretold the death of Jezebel, and appointed a king to a neighboring nation. In every way, Elijah was one of the greatest figures in the history of Israel.

The central core of Elijah's message was a call to return to the faith of Abraham, the true liberty of Moses, the covenant community and its law. Elijah evaluated the nation of his day and found it wanting. He demanded that those who bore the name of Israel should do the deeds of their fathers in faith. Some did. Some did not.

More prophets

The age of the prophet did not end with the exile in Babylon. Jesus was a prophet in the mold of Elijah as was his cousin, John the Baptist. Today, as in every age, there are prophets in the mold of Elijah, men and women calling not for new knowledge or understanding but for a return to the spirit that launched God's people on their ageless pilgrimage.

Few are called to be such prophets. It is enough to hear the voice of a prophet once or twice in a lifetime. But the responsibility of each person in the people of God is to respond to the prophet—to listen to his or her rebuke and to respond by a return to the primitive ideals which are our reason for existence.

Merely being a member of the people of God is not enough. It is not even enough to be both committed to the kingdom as was David and still skeptical of it as was Samuel. In addition, we must be willing to hear the voice of a new call to faith and so begin all over as Abraham did.

PONDERING POINT

Prophets are controversial people. Elijah was roundly hated by the court in Samaria. Elisha offended the ruling class of the Northern kingdom. Amos was the most indelicate of spokesmen for the Lord. His abrasiveness touched off controversy. Because the message of the prophets was so personal and so demanding, prophets were rejected and loved only from the distance of the centuries.

The greatest North American prophet was a man who brought to our consciousness the existence of our most serious social sin. He alerted us to the evil which lived in our own hearts and challenged us to do something about it. His voice rang in our ears and caused great pain, for its cutting edge brought strife into our calm possession of power over other people.

Our Century's Prophet

Dr. Lawrence Kohlberg called this man, "America's greatest moral educator." Presidents and politicians have lauded his impact upon our society. Churchmen have proclaimed him a voice crying in our American wilderness. Ordinary people have sensed that this man, for all his imperfections and they were many, spoke as did few others.

The man was Martin Luther King, Jr., who set in motion a whole series of reform movements in the United States, the most important of which was surely our confrontation with the great dilemma of our history, our racial attitudes. Few would call King a saint but most would see in him a great prophetic voice whose echoes are still with us.

PRIMARY LESSON PLAN

CLASS PLAN

Goal:

To show how we should react to our prophets.

Materials needed:

1) Copies, one per group of three, of the Task Sheet provided with this program. See page 137.
2) Pencil for each group
3) Blackboard, chalk and eraser
4) Newsprint, marking pen, masking tape
5) Bible

Methodology:

1. Using the Task Sheet, the student will identify prophets at work in our contemporary world.
2. The catechist, using the material from the Model Presentation, "Prophecy," will show how the prophets were at work in the history of God's people. Elijah will be used as an example.

Opening prayer:

(Jeremiah 1:4-8)

The following reading from the Book of Jeremiah records the prophet Jeremiah's call by God as a young man in 626 B.C.

The word of Yahweh was addressed to me, saying,

"Before I formed you in the womb I knew you,
before you came to birth I consecrated you,
I have appointed you as prophet to the nations."

I said, "Ah, Lord Yahweh; look, I do not know how to speak: I am a child!"

But Yahweh replied,
"Do not say, 'I am a child.'
Go now to those to whom I send you
and say whatever I command you.
Do not be afraid of them,
for I am with you to protect you—
it is Yahweh who speaks!"

Opening remarks:

Looking back over our unit so far, we talked about faith, then about the three consequences of faith—freedom, community and law. Later still, we talked about the attitudes we need to live in that community—criticism, cooperation, and a willingness to be somewhat lonely. Today we will look at prophets in a community—those special messengers of God who use hard-hitting words to demand that people remain faithful to their heritage.

Task sheet:

There are prophets in every age. Today, before we talk about the great prophet Elijah, we might well take a look at the people who are the prophets in our own age. Break into groups of three while I pass out the sheets and pencils. *(Read directions.)* Any questions?

Allow about 15 minutes.

Reporting:

(Use newsprint or blackboard.)

Now I'll ask each group to share one of its choices and tell us why you picked that person. *(Call on groups as time permits and list suggestions.)*

Discussion:

a) In which category did you have the most difficulty thinking of names? Why?
b) Did anyone strongly disagree with any of the names suggested? Why?
c) Would any of you like to be a prophet? Why?

SAVE POSTERS for the recap, Lesson 10.

Bridging:

With some understanding of the work of prophets in our own time, let's look back now at the greatest of the Old Testament prophets, Elijah.

Presentation:

Use the material from the Model Presentation, "Prophecy."

Discussion:

a) When Jesus asked his disciples, "Who do the crowds say I am?", they replied that some said he was Elijah. Why do you think people said that? (Luke 9:18-21)
b) Earlier, someone suggested that _____ was the greatest prophet of our time. How did/do people react to him/her?
c) Do you think we are usually comfortable around prophets? Why not?
d) Why is it so difficult to be corrected? What is our usual reaction? Why?

Closing prayer:

Read or have a student read: Mark 9:2-8, "The Transfiguration."

Bible References

The story of Elijah begins with chapter 17 of I Kings and continues through the first chapter of II Kings. To capture the flavor of the prophets you may also wish to read:

Elisha	II Kings 2-13
Amos	Amos 3-6
Hosea	Hosea 1-3
Micah	Micah 1-7

THE KINGDOM DIVIDED

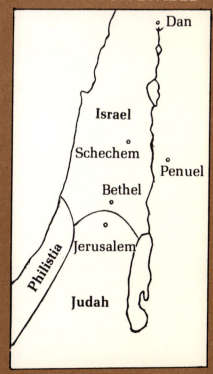

ALTERNATE PLAN

CLASS PLAN

Goal:
To show how we should react to our prophets.

Materials needed:
1) Bibles, one for each group of three. (Critical editions.)
2) Blank paper and pencil for each group of three
3) Blackboard, chalk and eraser
4) Newsprint, marking pen, masking tape

Methodology:
1. The students in groups of three will take one chapter from Matthew's gospel and trace through the references the allusions to the prophets.
2. The catechist will lead a discussion centering on the influence of the prophets on the thought of Jesus and the gospel writers, tying this in with the material from the Model Presentation, "Prophecy."

Opening prayer: (Luke 4:16-21)

(Jesus) came to Nazareth, where he had been brought up, and went into the synagogue on the sabbath day as he usually did. He stood up to read, and they handed him the scroll of the prophet Isaiah. Unrolling the scroll he found the place where it is written:

"The spirit of the Lord has been given to me,
for he has anointed me.
He has sent me to bring the good news to the poor,
to proclaim liberty to captives
and to the blind new sight,
to set the downtrodden free,
to proclaim the Lord's year of favour."

He then rolled up the scroll, gave it back to the assistant and sat down. And all eyes in the synagogue were fixed on him. Then he began to speak to them, "This text is being fulfilled even as you listen."

Opening comments:

In our day we use words like liberty, justice, family, friendship and loyalty without ever thinking where they came from. We take for granted most of our key ideas. This is always true of any civilization. The key ideas on which the civilization and culture rest are known but seldom discussed.

What is true of us was also true for Jesus. From the time he was a child, his ears were filled with the traditions of his people. Before anything else, Jesus was a Jewish man, one who was born into a long tradition. This tradition found its expression in the words of the prophets. Probably Jesus was able to quote much of the prophetic literature by heart, as were most of the young men of his age.

Research:

Today we are going to try to see the impact of all that tradition on the prophets on Jesus. Break into groups of three while I give each group a bible, paper and pencil.

Find Matthew's gospel. You will see, if you look closely, some strange little letters in the margins or in the footnotes. These abbreviations are for books of the bible. The numbers before

---

Excerpts from a great leader's moving address to the freedom-marchers

I say to you today, even though we face the difficulties of today and tomorrow, I still have a dream. It is a dream deeply rooted in the American Dream. I have a dream that one day this nation will rise up, live out the true meaning of its creed: "We hold these truths to be self-evident, that all men are created equal."

the colon stand for the chapter. The numbers after the colon stand for the verse. In the front of your bible the abbreviations are explained. Since we are looking for the influence of the prophets on Jesus, we'll just examine references from the books of the prophets. (List these on the blackboard or on newsprint. See Books of the Bible, page 62.)

I'll assign each group a different chapter of Matthew to research. Your task is to find each reference to one of the prophets. First write out the line in Matthew, then look up the Old Testament quote and write it opposite your quote from Matthew. You'll find it helpful to arrange your sheet of paper like this: *(Draw on the blackboard or newsprint to save for the recap.)*

Quote from Matthew	Quote from prophets
(Example) 1:23 The virgin will conceive and give birth to a son and they will call him Emmanuel,	Is. 7:14 The Lord himself, therefore, will give you a sign. It is this: the maiden is with child and will soon give birth to a son whom she will call Immanuel.

As you do this exercise, you will begin to see how almost every line of Matthew is filled with the thought of centuries past. Any questions? Let's begin. *Allow about 30 minutes.*

We'll discuss our research right after I share a few thoughts with you.

Catechist's presentation:

Here, the catechist may wish to review the Model Presentation, "Prophecy," or, if the class has not done the primary lesson, present the material for the first time. An introduction to a first time presentation:

Yes, Jesus was a man of the prophets, a man who knew the lore of his people. When Jewish people thought of heroes and of God they thought of the prophets. These great men were the messengers of God who kept calling His people back to the fervor of their original desert experience.

Discussion:

1. Was there one prophet whose name kept reappearing in your research? Who was mentioned most?
2. Does anyone know anything about this prophet? If not, where could we find a little information? *(Good sources, the introduction to the book in most translations, the paperback Dictionary of the Bible by John McKenzie, The New Catholic Encyclopedia.)*
3. Are there people alive today we think of as prophets? Who are they? Why do we consider them prophets?
4. Would you think of Martin Luther King Jr. as a prophet? Why? Why not? What about Pope John XXIII?

Closing prayer:

Let's listen very thoughtfully to the words of a man considered by many as one of the outstanding prophets of our time. (Martin Luther King, Jr.)

I have a dream that one day on the red hills of Georgia sons of former slaves and the sons of former slave-owners will be able to sit down together at the table of brotherhood. I have a dream that one day even the state of Mississippi, a state sweltering with the heat of injustice, sweltering with the heat of oppression, will be transformed into an oasis of freedom and justice.

I have a dream that my four little children will one day live in a nation where they will not be judged by the color of their skin but by the content of their character.

I have a dream that one day every valley shall be exalted, every hill and mountain shall be made low. The rough places will be made plain, and the crooked places will be made straight. This is the faith that I go back to the South with. With this faith we will be able to hew out of the mountain of despair a stone of hope. With this faith we will be able to work together, to pray together, to struggle together, to go to jail together, to stand up for freedom together, knowing we will be free one day.

This will be the day when all of God's children will be able to sing with new meaning, "let freedom ring." So let freedom ring from the prodigious hilltops of New Hampshire. Let freedom ring from the mighty mountains of New York. But not only that. Let freedom ring from Stone Mountain of Georgia. Let freedom ring from every hill and molehill of Mississippi, from every mountain side.

When we allow freedom to ring—when we let it ring from every city and every hamlet, from every state and every city, we will be able to speed up that day when all of God's children, black men and white men, Jews and Gentiles, Protestants and Catholics, will be able to join hands and sing in the words of the old Negro spiritual, "Free at last, Free at last, Great God a-mighty. We are free at last."

MINI LESSON PLANS

The purpose of the ideas which follow is to provide the creative teacher with further suggestions for classroom experiences related to the original Model Presentation.

Filmstrip Study

This is especially easy with the subject of prophets. Teleketics, 1229 South Santee Street, Los Angeles, CA 90015, has four filmstrips called *Indian Viewpoints* which portray prophetic leadership among the American Indian people. These provide an excellent comparison with the prophets of Israel's past.

The Thomas Klise (Box 3418, Peoria, IL 61614) series *Images of the New Man* has a good filmstrip on Martin Luther King, Jr., surely one of the prophets of our day. Klise also produces a filmstrip called, *All Doctrine Is Social Doctrine* which is itself a strong prophetic statement to contemporary Catholics.

Cathedral Films, whose products may be ordered through Roa Films, 1696 North Astor Street, Milwaukee, WI 53202, has ten filmstrips on the prophets packaged in two series *Story of the Prophets 1* and *2*. This is the best source of historical perspective.

Most of these filmstrips can be borrowed from your diocesan filmstrip depository.

Role Playing

Elijah and the Prophets of Baal is a dramatic story recounted in 18th chapter of I Kings. Students can be asked to imagine a television news team is reporting the incident and write the script, devise appropriate interviews with such contemporaries as King Ahab, Queen Jezebel, Elisha, Jehu, and the widow of Zarephath. When all the parts of the program have been pieced together, it can be presented to other classes or to a parents' group.

Imagine A Prophet

Imagine a prophet today in your city. Ask the class to give the prophet a name and a specific mission. Then, assign different groups the task of writing newspaper accounts of his exploits, the reception he is given, the reaction of the town's leaders, the resistance of the people, etc. When the newspaper has been completed, ask the students to find similarities between what they have imagined and the stories of the Old Testament prophets and Jesus himself, who was often called a prophet.

Research Prophets

The prophetic story is a fascinating one. Using the guide on page 138 have students research several of the prophets and report their findings to the class. As they report point out patterns and divergences in the lives of these great men.

TASK SHEET 8 (Duplicator master of this sheet in packet)

PROPHETS

A prophet is one who speaks the truth for God. He calls people from their laziness and evil ways to live lives which are in keeping with our highest ideals.

In the spaces below try to discover men and women who have been or who are prophets in different areas of life.

In our country   **Reasons for your choice**

1. _____

2. _____

3. _____

In your own town

1. _____

2. _____

3. _____

In your school

1. _____

2. _____

3. _____

Among teenagers

1. _____

2. _____

3. _____

Who do you think has been the greatest prophet in the world during the 20th century and why?

_____
_____
_____
_____

The Old Testament Prophet

The Idea of the Prophet

The prophet was originally an ecstatic who spoke messages which were believed to be from God. He seems to have had no official position in Israel but was listened to because of the popular belief that he delivered God's word. Thus, we read of Saul's seeking out the prophet Samuel to discover the whereabouts of his father's lost animals.

In time, especially after Solomon's days, the prophet was regarded as a private citizen who called for the downfall of the monarchy. Thus Elisha was willing to work with the pagan king Hazael to insure the downfall of his own kingdom of Israel, so convinced was he that the monarchy was opposed to the worship of the true God.

Prophets abounded during the lifetime of the two kingdoms and even through the exile in Babylon. Their main task was to recall Israel to the fervor of its early belief in the Lord. After the exile, the place of the prophets seems to have been taken by the scribes and writers. What prophets there were provided only a shadow of the earlier greats.

It is interesting to note that both John the Baptist and Jesus were thought of as prophets by their contemporaries.

Some of the Great Prophets

Elijah called Israel to renew its faith in the Lord. He predicted a period of drought, prayed for its end, rebuked the king for his greed, schemed with foreigners against the unjust king, met God in a beautifully described mystical experience and left behind a group of prophets with their own leader, Elisha. Elijah was taken into heaven in a fiery chariot and was expected to return just before the Christ. John the Baptist is often considered a later day Elijah.

Elisha was called from the fields by Elijah to be his successor and to receive his mantle and "a double portion of his spirit." The stories about Elisha are marked by marvels. Some of them seem to be an imitation of the earlier stories of Elijah. Elisha stood for simplicity of life and for complete dependence upon the Lord.

Amos, Hosea and Micah were probably contemporaries, all speaking about 750 B.C. Amos was a rude shepherd and a tender of fig trees. His message was directed against a corrupt monarchy and the court which gathered around it. Hosea was an unusual man, deeply in love with a faithless woman whom he accepted back after her infidelities. He spoke of God as a faithful husband and Israel as the faithless wife. His prophecy is marked with great tenderness. Micah proclaimed political disaster for those who would not worship properly. He scolded the Hebrews for their oppression of the poor, their dishonesty and their worship of idols.

Isaiah, Jeremiah, Ezekiel are all prophets who spoke during the last days of either Israel or Judah. Isaiah probably spoke about 700 B.C., Jeremiah about 600 B.C. and Ezekiel about the same time. All called the people back to the worship of the one God. The books which bear their names are probably compilations of their messages blended with later Hebrew thought.

9 New Theologies

CATECHIST'S BACKGROUND

Faith and knowledge

The act of faith is more than knowledge. When people believe in the Lord, their whole humanity is involved in that act—intellect, emotions, body and even their other human relationships. Faith is more than knowing. It is the gift of one person's total self to another. Involved with this act of faith is a trust and a love. We do not believe in one we cannot trust or love. For this reason the three theological virtues—faith, hope and charity are always united, at least in this life.

Knowledge about God and religious things is not nearly so involving as is faith. Knowledge is primarily an act of our intellect. Knowledge is the assembly of facts about God and an attempt to see the relationship among them. While such an enterprise may have its emotional and even physical effects upon the person who pursues it, knowledge remains primarily a work of the mind. It does not exact from the one who pursues it the same kind of total commitment that faith demands.

Israel was always a people of faith. In the desert, Moses asked and received from the people an act of trusting, loving faith in the Lord. Their knowledge of this Lord was limited to the new revelation of his name, Yahweh, and to his intervention into their own history. Who or what he might be other than these few clues, the Israelite people did not know. They were a simple tribal people not much given to abstract speculation.

Development of dogma

As Israel lived out its mission through many generations, Hebrew thinkers amassed an ever greater knowledge of this God they believed in. At first, their knowledge was quite primitive by our standards. In time, this knowledge took on a surprising sophistication.

In the beginning, the Lord was seen as Israel's God. Only slowly did it appear that this Lord was also the Lord of heaven and earth, the one God of all. Slowly, too, people began to ask where this God had come from, who had brought Him into being. The thinkers answered that this God had always been. He was the beginning of all things other than Himself. Thinkers also added the notion that just as He had always been so He would always be. Thus, the idea of eternity was born.

People wondered, too, about evil in the world. Where did it come from? Had God created evil? If so, why? Theologians pondered this problem for centuries and decided that indeed evil did exist, but that God had not created it. Nor, were they willing to grant, did any other god or demigod. This was the answer common among pagan thinkers of the time. Instead, the thinkers of Israel placed the responsibility for evil not on the shoulders of some spirit of evil but on humankind. Man and woman were the authors of evil. What God created was good.

People wondered, too, about the future. What would happen to those who lived the good life, who were faithful to the covenant? This problem was one of Israel's most difficult ones. At first, the promise of progeny was sufficient to assuage people's desire for some continuity with the future.

Later, quite late in fact, Jewish thinkers began to move toward the idea of a life after death, a life in which the good were finally rewarded and the evil finally punished. The Book of Job shows the anguish sensitive people brought to the solution of this problem.

Another problem which haunted the Jewish culture was the punishment for a parent's sin? Some writers believed He did, others would not accept such a vision of God. This problem remained unresolved even in Jesus' day.

These are but a few examples of the development of Hebrew thought through the Old Testament. Countless examples of this development can be given in the moral order, too. Mass murder, polygamy and slavery were all permitted at one time or other in Old Testament history. Only gradually did these acts come to be regarded as less than perfectly in tune with living the covenant relationship.

Israel was a living people, a people constantly challenged by the forces of history, constantly developing its own understanding of the meaning of life. It is a mistaken notion that the people of the desert days had the pure idea of the Lord which became adulterated as years wore on. The desert people did aspire to a purity of faith as did Israelites of every generation. Yet, it was subsequent generations which brought greater knowledge and understanding to this faith. While faith remained a mystical and undefined element of Israel's history, knowledge can be measured. Our measurements show us quite clearly that Israel grew in knowledge as she grew in age.

The theological voices

After the fall of Jerusalem in 587 B.C., the harsh voices of the prophets were seldom heard. Their message had been preserved. Every adult Hebrew knew their warnings and took heed of them as best he could. What was needed in the second half of Israel's history was deeper thought about the mystery of their faith rather than a call to rekindle it.

The Old Testament books composed during this period are filled with such a search for knowledge. The Book of Job comes to grips with the problem of the suffering among those who live good lives. The Book of Wisdom attempts to show how one lives out the covenant life in polite society. The Book of Qoheleth (Ecclesiastes) comments on the vanity in human life and its ultimate meaning.

In the final chapters of Isaiah (chapters added by an unknown hand), the author tells some of the most insightful stories of the meaning of Israel and the covenant vocation. Here he glorifies suffering for the Lord and promises the reader a final restoration of justice in the world. The opening chapters of the Book of Genesis, relying on ancient traditions, were resculptured at this time to answer questions like the purpose of life, the place of God in it, the relationship of man and woman, and many other profound theological questions.

During the centuries which passed, from the restoration of Jerusalem until the coming of Jesus, the Jewish mind was at work searching for an ever deeper understanding of the implications of faith in the Lord. Scholars today still stand in amazement at the depth and scholarship of these early thinkers. In many areas their ideas remain our best solutions for crucial problems of life and its meaning.

Pedagogy

In this lesson we have attempted to show how the later books of the Old Testament open us to an understanding of the theological enterprise in today's Church. The **Primary Lesson Plan** asks students to compare the new folk music with traditional hymnology to get a picture of changes in the Church. The **Model Presentation** shows how similar changes were initiated by the writers of many late Old Testament books. The **Alternate Lesson Plan** has students compare the popular teachings of the Church in the pre-Vatican era with contemporary teaching on several important topics.

The **Mini Lesson Plans** suggest a study of Second Isaiah, a discussion of theologians and their role in the Church, a discussion with a professional theologian, and also suggests several possible filmstrips for viewing.

The **Catechist Resource Sheet** contains a list of some of the most honored theologians in our Catholic tradition.

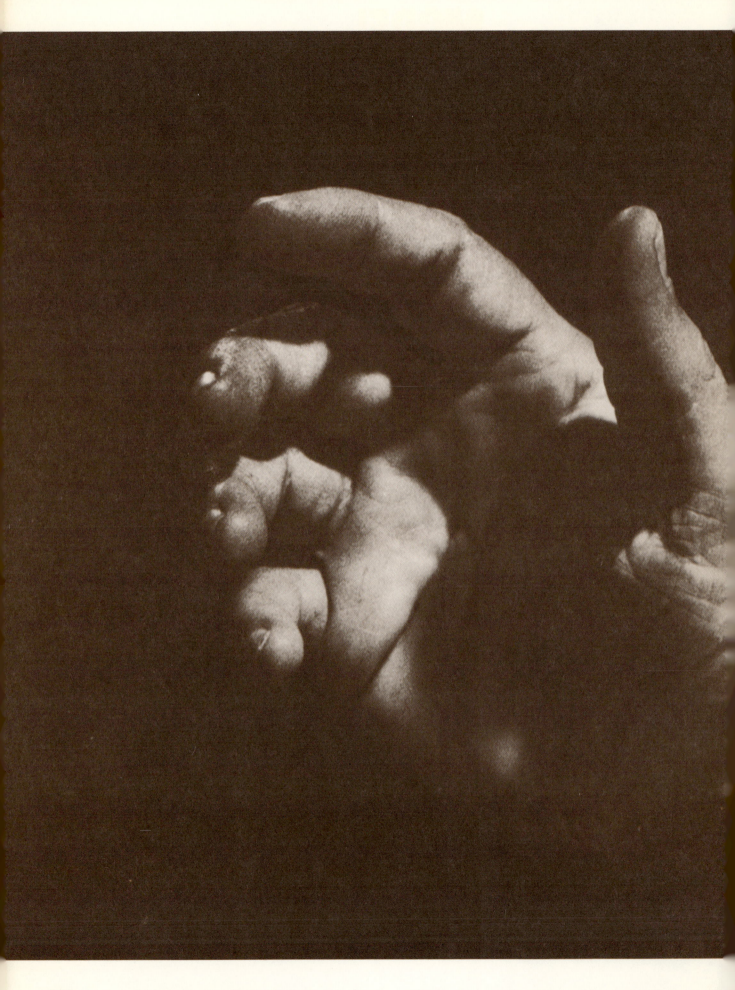

MODEL PRESENTATION

"New Theologies"

Topics to be presented:

1. Parts of Isaiah and the early chapters of Genesis provided Israel with profound theological insights.
2. Job, Jonah and other later Old Testament books show how the thought of Israel developed.
3. Today's theologians help us deepen our understanding of the mysteries revealed by God.

A new kind of prophet

During our quiet moments we often ask profound questions, questions about God, about the meaning of life, what happens after death and who we really are. During and after the exile in Babylon, a new kind of prophet arose in Israel—men with a message not only about the here and now realities of faith, as Elijah had provided, but men who went beyond the everyday thoughts of their people to answer people's deepest questioning.

These men were a group we today would call the theologians, those who thought not so much about the day-to-day realities of life as about the reasons behind them. These were the men who opened new vistas of understanding and who deepened the vision of God available to His people. Sometimes these men are referred to as prophets and sometimes simply as scribes or writers.

Isaiah and Genesis

The deepest of all these reflections is to be found in two sources, the second part of the Book of Isaiah and the first chapters of the Book of Genesis.

We do not know who wrote this second part of the Book of Isaiah. Most scholars today feel certain that Isaiah, the eighth century B.C. prophet, was not himself the author. Rather, an obscure hand has traced some of the most sublime ideas about Israel, its heritage, and its meanings for the world and added them to Isaiah's earlier writings. The words of this section of Isaiah were often on the lips of Jesus himself.

At a time when the Jewish people were humiliated by their slavery in Babylon, this great genius opened a whole new understanding of what it meant to be a child of Abraham. Not until the coming of Saint Paul was there to be so fertile and so imaginative a voice in Israel.

Like the writer of the second part of the Book of Isaiah, the writers of the early chapters of Genesis are unknown to us. Scholars tell us that sometime around the Babylonian exile a group of scribes and priests assembled the oral and written traditions of the Jewish people and added to these traditions ideas of their own. This poetry and parable in Genesis provided the common people, in language they could understand, a message about man, about Israel, and about the whole interaction of God and His people.

Job, Jonah and Wisdom

There were other writers in this period, too. We are familiar with the patience of Job. The Book of Job was written to help people understand the need for a theology of afterlife to explain the apparent injustice in the world. Then there was the story of Jonah and the whale, a parable about Israel's timidity and lack of faith in crisis. And there was the brilliant story of Daniel's many exploits, which encouraged and gave meaning to the Jews of a later date who were suffering under the persecutive boot of the Seleucid empire.

And there were the more obvious wisdom writers—the author of the Wisdom of Solomon, Ecclesiastes with its ironic if not tragic view of human life, and Proverbs, a book about behaving properly in polite Jewish society. All these were lesser books, perhaps, but necessary for the overall meaning system that Jesus was initiated into and on which he built his understanding of the world and of his Father.

In our day, too, there are writers and scribes. There are men and women who open up insights into what it means to be human and what it means to be part of the growing kingdom of God. Like the men of old, they manage somehow to take what is best from the culture around them and to give it intense meaning for the people of God.

Today's theologians

These writers and scribes are the theologians of our day. When we talk of the profound impact of the Second Vatican Council on the life of the church, we seldom think of the basis of that council. It was a whole new vision of the mission of the church and a whole new way of thinking about Jesus and his Father. The vision did not come directly and immediately from the bishops at the council but was adopted by them from the writings of influential theologians.

One of those men was the Dominican theologian, Father Yves Congar, whose return to the early sense of Christianity had been scoffed at and even angrily suppressed at times. Yet, when the council fathers looked for some new ways to understand church, they looked at this simple priest whose writing spanned half a century. It was his understanding and the understanding of others like him which made it possible to reform and renew the church.

In secular life, too, we have our theorists. One who has had a profound impact on our world is a Scottish economist named Keynes who created a whole new vision of what the economy of a nation was all about. Presidents and congressmen have, sometimes without knowing it, taken Keynes' meaning system and put it into practice in the world.

Again, few of us are called to be theologians, to break new ground and create new understandings. But all of us, like the people of the Old Testament, are called to listen to new thought and to respond to it creatively.

PONDERING POINT

John Courtney Murray

Theology is by and large a dry science whose battles are fought in classrooms and learned journals. Seldom does the work of a theologian win wide acceptance in his or her own lifetime. The story of the great Jesuit theologian, John Courtney Murray, is a happy exception.

Until Vatican II, most Catholic theologians taught that the ideal political situation was a Catholic government which actively promoted the Catholic vision of life. They believed that the truth had its own rights and those who sinned against the truth should be restrained from contaminating others with their error. This view was as old as the Middle Ages, possibly much older.

The American experience of pluralism went counter to this old wisdom. In the United States, the government championed no religion but did provide religious freedom to all. John Courtney Murray, himself an American, sensed that this system was a better one. He reasoned that the rights of individuals to decide upon the truth was prior to any right of truth itself.

For a long generation Murray's thought was condemned by traditional thinkers. He was accused of being out of touch with the Catholic tradition. He was said to be undermining the great religio-political synthesis of Catholic thought. At best, he was a suspect member of the Church.

At Vatican II, the bishops of the world took up the problem Murray had raised in theological circles and declared that Murray, not the traditionalists, was correct. Within his own lifetime this great Jesuit theologian had seen his thought, once termed radical and dangerous, become the accepted norm for Catholics throughout the world.

PRIMARY LESSON PLAN

CLASS PLAN

Goal:
To show how we should react to our theologians.

Materials needed:
1) Copies, one per group of three, of the Task Sheet provided with this program. See page 153.
2) Blank paper and pencil for each student
3) Blackboard, chalk and eraser
4) Newsprint, marking pen, masking tape
5) Recommended: record player, recordings of folk, traditional, and Gregorian Chant hymns.
6) Missalettes

Methodology:
1. Using the Task Sheet, the students will study the major change in church music, from the traditional hymns to the folk hymns.
2. The catechist, using the material from the Model Presentation, "New Theologies," will show that Isaiah and other great minds in the Old Testament gave the Jewish people whole new ways of looking at things, opening doors closed for many years.

Opening prayer: (Isaiah 45:9-12)

This reading from Isaiah is what we today call a theological reflection. It attempts to explain man's relationship with God.

Can it argue with the man who fashioned it,
one vessel among earthen vessels?
Does the clay say to its fashioner, "What are you making?",
does the thing he shaped say, "You have no skill"?
Woe to him who say to a father, "What have you begotten?"
or to a woman, "To what have you given birth?"

Thus says Yahweh,
the Holy One, he who fashions Israel:
Is it for you to question me about my children
and to dictate to me what my hands should do?
I it was who made the earth,
and created man who is on it.
I it was who spread out the heavens with my hands
and now give orders to their whole array.

Opening remarks:

Last time we talked about the prophets—those voices which recalled Israel to their old and correct ways, to their faith, their freedom, covenant and law. Today we will be talking about some different prophets—men who opened up new ways of thinking about the covenant, the law and the experience of freedom.

In order to get some feeling of how one person can open up a whole new way of thinking and feeling, let's take a look at something which is happening right now as a result of a single person daring to think that church music could be like folk music. Up until about ten or twelve years ago, no one used a guitar in the church—no one. Father Clarence Rivers, a young black priest, suggested that guitar music was good church music. Then, things began to change. His way of thinking opened up new doors to everyone in the church.

Task sheet:

Break into groups of three and look at today's task sheet. *(Pass out sheets and pencils.)* You are asked to describe the differences among the three kinds of church music. *(If possible, play selections of each type—folk, traditional, Gregorian. Or, give each group a copy of the monthly missalette which contains selections which are folk or traditional. You will need to describe Gregorian Chant—In Latin, sung in a solemn tone.) Allow 15-20 minutes.*

Reporting: *(Use newsprint or blackboard.)*

a. Will a group volunteer to describe the differences in the rhythm between the three types of church music? *(List descriptions.)* Does anyone wish to add to our list? *Repeat process for words, melody, people's response and subjects.*
b. Now, who will share a response to the question: "In what ways did Father Rivers and his followers give Catholics a whole new way of thinking about church music?" *(List responses.)*

Discussion:

a) Which type of church music do you prefer and why? *(Call on volunteers.)*
b) Do you think folk music changed people's way of thinking about God? Why?

Bridging:

Music is just one way of experiencing a change. More important are whole new ways of understanding life. The man who wrote the second part of the Book of Isaiah was an initiator of new understandings of life. Before I share a few ideas with you, take out a piece of paper and pencil and write: "We need theologians because . . ."

Presentation: Use the material from the Model Presentation, "New Theologies."

Discussion:

a) What impressed you most about what I just said?
b) Who will share his or her completion of the reflection: "We need theologians because . . ."?
c) Can you think of any New Testament theologians? Any contemporary theologians?
d) Who, more than anyone else, can help you understand what life is about? Why?

Closing prayer: (Isaiah 42:1-4)

Here is my servant whom I uphold,
my chosen one in whom my soul delights.
I have endowed him with my spirit
that he may bring true justice to the nations.

He does not cry out or shout aloud,
or make his voice heard in the streets.
He does not break the crushed reed,
nor quench the wavering flame.

Faithfully he brings true justice;
he will neither waver, nor be crushed
until true justice is established on earth,
for the islands are awaiting his law.

Bible References

The four most beautiful passages in the Book of Isaiah are probably 42:1-7, 49:1-9, 50:4-9, and 52:13-53:12. You may also enjoy reading:

Jeremiah 1 and 2

Jeremiah 30 and 31

Ezekiel 1-2:21

Genesis 1-12

ALTERNATE PLAN

CLASS PLAN

Goal:
To show how we should react to our theologians.

Materials needed:
1) Blackboard, chalk and eraser
2) Newsprint, marking pen, tape
3) If music is used for prayer, necessary equipment or guitarist and songbooks.

Methodology:
1. The catechist will share with the students the way in which his or her own perception of religion and life has changed since Vatican II. Or, if the catechist does not feel able to do this, he/she will invite a guest speaker.
2. The students will dialogue with the speaker in order to understand more clearly how the changes took place. This will serve as a prelude to studying or reviewing the role of the great theologian-prophets.

Advance preparation:
1. If the catechist prefers bringing in a guest speaker, he/she should select someone (a priest perhaps) who is knowledgeable, an interesting speaker, and able to communicate well with teenagers.
2. A guest speaker should be invited well in advance and furnished with a copy of the instructions for the speaker below.

Opening prayer: (Matthew 7:7-12.)

When Jesus was teaching the crowds on the mountainside, he said:
> "Ask and it will be given to you; search, and you will find; knock, and the door will be opened to you. For the one who asks always receives; the one who searches always finds; the one who knocks will always have the door opened to him. Is there a man among you who would hand his son a stone when he asked for bread? Or would you hand him a snake when he asked for a fish? If you, then, who are evil, know how to give your children what is good, how much more will your Father in heaven give good things to those who ask him!
> "So always treat others as you would like them to treat you; that is the meaning of the Law and the Prophets."

Opening comments:

Since the Second Vatican Council which took place during the early 1960's, the way we Catholic people look at religion and life has changed dramatically. It is not one particular thing or another that has changed, but our whole way of life.

You probably have heard of Vatican II, as it was called. It is known as the council that put the Mass into English, or perhaps, the council which led to changing the age-old custom of not eating meat on Friday. But, there was so much more than this.

Presentation on changes:

Today I *(or the guest)* would like to tell you how the way we look at life as Catholics has changed. On newsprint *(or the blackboard)*

I have placed a diagram which will be the outline of what I have to say. After I have talked about each item, I hope you will question me or share stories.

Instructions for the speaker:

1. Before class put the following outline on the blackboard or newsprint to save for the recap, Lesson 10. If this outline does not seem to fit your experience, change it so that it does. What is important is your own experience.

	Pre-Vatican II	Post-Vatican II
God		
Religion		
Church		
Mass		
Prayer		
Jesus		
Morals		
Priest (Sister, Teacher)		
Religious education		
Laity		
Rules		

2. Prepare ahead so that you can tell not only the way things were and are with you but also anecdotes which illustrate the more subjective concepts.
3. After each of the items in the outline, invite the students to talk freely. Use such questions as the following to stimulate discussion:
    a. Does the way we used to think seem strange to you today? Why? Why not?
    b. Have your parents ever told you stories like these? Will you share them with us?
    c. Which way, the older or the newer, seems better to you and why?
    d. Have you any idea why this particular change took place?
4. When you have completed the whole presentation, ask the following or similar questions:
    a. Why do you think the Church has councils?
    b. Do you think change is good for the Church? Bad? Why?

Catechist's presentation:

An alternative to the usual presentation by the catechist, especially if the catechist has given the presentation in the primary lesson, would be to have a student make the presentation, using the material from "New Theologies." Be sure to appoint the student well in advance and insist upon a thorough presentation. Never allow anyone to read the essay aloud to the class.
An introduction to a first time presentation:
Many times in the history of God's people, ways of looking at things have changed. Back in Old Testament days there were many men who opened the Jewish people to whole new ways of looking at things.

Closing prayer:

If possible, sing together "The New Creation" with guitar accompaniment. Otherwise, select one of the prayers not used in an earlier lesson.

MINI LESSON PLANS

The purpose of the ideas which follow is to provide the creative teacher with further suggestions for classroom experiences related to the original Model Presentation.

The Book of Isaiah

This book is among the most beautiful in the Old Testament. Chapters 40 through 55, often called Second Isaiah or The Book of the Consolation of Israel, is possibly Isaiah's most outstanding section. A worthwhile project for a class would be to outline this section showing in detail the topics the author thought important enough for the people of the day to mention repeatedly. In a discussion students might then compare the concerns of people of Isaiah's day with those of their own.

Theologians

Theologians through the ages is the topic of the page which follows. On this page are mentioned some of the greatest of the Christian thinkers. Individual students might be assigned the task of researching and reporting on the lives and works of some of these great men and women. Reports by several students with questions and answers from the class would make a lively lesson. See page 154.

Invitation

Invite a theologian to the classroom for dialogue with the students. Most Catholic colleges have a theological faculty. Many parish priests and religious education directors are quite competent in theology. The teacher should help students formulate questions beforehand to ask during the discussion. Some important questions surely will be: 1) How do theologians decide what questions they will try to answer? 2) Where do theologians look for answers to their questions? 3) What questions are the most talked about ones today.

Filmstrip Studies in Theology

There is a wide variety of filmstrips appropriate to this area of study.

The Story of the Prophets I and II, mentioned in lesson 8, pg. 00, has episodes on the prophetic theologians mentioned in this lesson.

Teleketics, 1229 South Santee Street, Los Angeles, CA 90015, has a very sensitive filmstrip, *In Search of God*, which sets the scene for the theological inquiry.

Thomas S. Klise, Box 3418, Peoria, Il 61614, has several appropriate filmstrips: *Understanding Genesis*, a two part filmstrip which will help the student grasp the literary form and the questions raised and answered in Genesis; *The Book of Job*, a good explanation of the problems raised in this remarkable Old Testament book; and *Images of the Future*, an eight filmstrip series which attempts to cope with the problems of our technological future from a Christian perspective. These filmstrips are really theology themselves.

Most of these filmstrips should be available to the teacher at the diocesan filmstrip depository.

TASK SHEET 9 (Duplicator master of this sheet in packet)

The Beat

About ten years ago a young black priest, Father Clarence Rivers, brought folk music to the Catholic church. Soon, many others followed his lead so that today almost all churches have folk music at some of their services.

A. Directions: Try to compare folk music with the regular hymn music used in church and (if you have ever heard it) the official church music, Gregorian chant.

Item	Folk	Hymns	Chant
Rhythm			
Words			
Melody			
People's response			
Subjects			

B. In what ways did Father Rivers and his followers give Catholics a whole new way of thinking about church music?

1. _____
2. _____
3. _____

_____
_____
_____
_____
_____

CATECHIST RESOURCE SHEET

The Catholic Theological Story

1. Earliest Writers

The first Christian writers were concerned with the problem of Christian survival in a hostile Roman Empire. They wrote to defend their understanding of Christianity against the dominant pagans and against aberrations of all kinds within the church. Saint Ignatius of Antioch, Saint Irenaeus, Saint Cyprian, Tertullian, and the unknown writer of the *Didache,* a small book of liturgy and practice dating from the first century, are important names in this era.

2. Trinitarian Writers

No sooner had the church been freed to practice in the empire than a great controversy arose over the proper way to speak about the Trinity. Saint Gregory Nazianzen, Saint John Chrysostom, and many others clarified this topic.

3. The Last Romans

In the century before the end of the Roman Empire a great number of highly talented men wrote about a variety of theological problems. Saint Jerome wrote about the bible and translated it. Saint Cyril of Alexandria continued the trinitarian clarification. Saint Ambrose wrote of the spiritual life. And the great Saint Augustine left a legacy of theology which is still read and is still influential.

4. Quiet Period

During the centuries between the fall of the Roman Empire and the rise of the medieval civilization, the church was attempting to preserve knowledge rather than to expand it. Saint Gregory the Great, Beothius, Saint Bede, and Saint John Damascene were important writers of this period.

5. The Scholastic Flowering

During the 10th to the 14th centuries Europe witnessed the growth of Catholicism's most important theological period. Discovery of Greek thought and the availability of the works of the past set the stage for some of our greatest thinkers. Peter Abelard, Peter Lombard, Gratian, and Saint Bernard of Clairvaux were early leaders. Most of their work was organization of existing knowledge. They were followed by the greats of our tradition: Saint Albertus Magnus, Saint Thomas Aquinas, Saint Bonaventure, Duns Scotus, Roger Bacon, Alexander of Hales, and lesser lights such as Jacob Voragine. These men attempted to synthesize Greek philosophy and Christian revelation.

6. The Catholic Reformation

The initiative in theology passed from the Catholic church to the new Protestant thinkers. Most of the Catholic theology of the 16th through the 19th centuries was defensive in the face of Protestant challenges. Cajetan, Suarez, Saint Peter Canesius, Saint Robert Bellarmine and many others gave the Catholic position a strong base during the Reformation controversy. Others turned from controversy to the mystical life. Saint Teresa, Saint John of the Cross, Saint Ignatius, Blaise Pascal, Saint Alphonsus and others wrote of the personal relationship to God.

7. Forerunners of Vatican II

For a century before Vatican II thinkers were trying to relate the church to the new technological world. Among these were Mathias Scheeben, Jacques Maritain, and Yves Congar.

8. Contemporary Thinkers

Today's Church is filled with creative thinkers, all attempting to bring order and understanding to the explosive world in which we live. Some of the most popular voices are: Hans Kung, the German who has tried to bring the insights of Protestant theology to Catholics, Bernard Lonergan, the great expounder of Saint Thomas Aquinas, Bernard Haring, the most influential moral theologian, and Karl Rahner, the German who is perhaps the most read of all contemporary writers of Catholic theology.

Some significant American voices are: John L. McKenzie, Raymond Brown, and Barnabas Ahearn on scripture, Gregory Baum on ecumenical theology, Charles Curran on moral theology, and Rosemary Reuther and Avery Dulles on speculative theology.

The most vital theological input today seems to be coming from Latin America with its theology of liberation formulated by such people as Gustavo Gutierrez.

10 The Recap

PRIMARY LESSON PLAN

CLASS PLAN

Goal:

To help the students review and evaluate the topics covered and the discussions held during this unit.

Materials needed:

1) Copies, one per student, of "An Old Testament Prayer," for which a duplicator master is provided with this program
2) A bible for each group
3) Nine large pieces of newsprint or posterboard, masking tape
4) Marking pens and glue for each group
5) Copy of each of the nine resource essays. Teacher may xerox copies or cut them from this book
6) Copy of each of the task sheets and research sheets used in class
7) Copy of the goal for each lesson.
8) Notes taken during each class discussion (newsprint or student notebook.) See instructions on page 11.
9) "Sabbath Prayer" from Fiddler On The Roof, record player.

Methodology:

1. Students will be divided into nine groups. Each group will review one of the topics covered and prepare a word collage containing the main ideas of the topic.
2. Students will study all nine collages in silence.
3. Students will be invited to vote and discuss these lessons under categories given by the catechist.

Opening prayer:

Students will be given copies of "An Old Testament Prayer" and be asked to recite it together, slowly and with feeling. A period of meditation may follow.

Opening comments:

For the past several meetings we have been researching and discussing some of the great personalities of the Old Testament. From their experiences of life and God we have gleaned lessons for our own lives. Today we will be reviewing all this information in order to try to see the big picture, the whole of which each of these people was a part.

    I will divide the class into nine groups *(or individuals if the class is small)*. Each group will be responsible for making a word collage about one of the topics we covered. *(Assign each group a different lesson.)* To help you remember what we talked about and what material we covered, I have for each group:

The goal for your topic
A copy of the task sheet and/or the study sheet used
A copy of the catechist's Model Presentation from which I took
    much of my presentation
A bible to help you look up any references
Notes from class discussions

Notes from any Mini Lessons used
Large posterboard or newsprint
Marking pens, glue

Look over the material and on your piece of posterboard or newsprint jot down key words which help you recall the highlights of our discussions and/or my presentation. You may wish to incorporate your task sheets and notes into the design of your collage. Perhaps you will want to add an appropriate quotation from the bible.

When the rest of us look at your word collage we should remember much of the lesson with little or no effort.

If everyone understands, let's begin.

Allow 30 minutes for the project.

Discussion:

First, let's spend ten minutes just looking at the collages. I will ask you to maintain silence as you move from one to another thinking about the lessons we covered earlier. When we are finished I will be asking you several questions about them, like which lesson was most helpful, which was most interesting, etc.

Allow ten minutes for viewing.

Now that we have looked over the collages, let's discuss this unit.

1. Which of the nine topics did you find personally most helpful? *(Encourage discussion and at the end of the discussion take a vote.)*
2. Which of the nine topics covered did you find the most interesting? Why? *(Discussion. Vote.)*
3. Which of the nine topics did you find the most confusing? Why? *(Discussion. Vote.)*
4. If you were going to give the Sunday sermon on one of these topics, which one would you use? Why? *(Discussion. Vote.)*
5. What character in these topics do you think was most like people today? Why? *(Discussion. Vote.)*
6. If you could live in Old Testament times, what era would you like to live in? Why? *(Discussion. Vote.)*

Reflection:

(At this point the catechist may wish to share with the class his/her own feelings about the unit, the attention given it by the students, the strengths and weaknesses of the material, etc.)

Closing prayer:

Play "Sabbath Prayer" from Fiddler On The Roof, or use a prayer from the lesson the students found most helpful.

Experiential Living and Learning

An Old Testament Weekend

Why have a weekend program?

Religious education has a two-fold goal: 1) the creation of situations which lead to the possibility of personal faith experience, and 2) the systematic presentation of the history, beliefs and values of the Roman Catholic Church. The two goals are by no means mutually exclusive. In fact, they should reinforce each other.

Classroom experiences are, then, more than formal instruction. They have about them the almost indefinable invitation to faith. But the weekend experience is much more suitable for the faith experience. The blocks of time given over to the Lord are longer, the companionship more intense, and the atmosphere more relaxed.

How to prepare for a weekend

The first item on the organizer's agenda is the formation of a group of adults who will make the weekend with the youngsters. This is the crucial step in the process. These people should have strong personalities who can by their own example and personality set the proper tone for the experience. They may be quite young—college age even, or older—even parents of the students. Choose people who have a strong personal faith and are able to relate easily to teenagers. Avoid those who are afraid to correct improper conduct and those who are overly authoritarian. People on both extremes of this continuum will damage the spirit of the weekend.

Once this group has been formed and has prayed together about the weekend, ask them to answer the following questions:

1. What weekend will be most convenient for the greatest number of the teenagers? Consult the teens themselves and also consult the local school schedule for football games, tournaments, etc.
2. Where can the weekend be held? A retreat house is ideal but a summer cottage will do for a small group. Do not overlook Boy Scout, Girl Scout, and other youth facilities which are often available at a modest fee.
3. How will transportation be provided? It is always a good thing to provide the transportation yourselves and keep the group without the option to drive off during the evening.
4. Who will arrange parent permission? Usually a note for parents is required by most schools or parishes and their insurance companies. Check with the principal, pastor or D.R.E. for any specifics.
5. How will the group be fed? Cooking your own food can be a real community builder, although it will require a patient adult.
6. How will the weekend be financed? Will students pay or will the school or parish pick up the bill or will the costs be split? Will there be provision for students who cannot afford to pay?
7. What will the Schedule be? *(See the next section for ideas.)*

What to do during the weekend?

The following ideas are grouped under three headings: 1) prayer, 2) community building, and 3) instruction.

1. Ideas for prayer experiences

Since the group has just studied the Old Testament, the many beautiful prayers provided with the lessons can be excellent opportunities for prayer.

a. Quiet time: schedule several 20-minute periods in which all activity and all conversation is suspended. Mimeograph or duplicate some of the prayers from the lessons and give them to the youngsters and adults. Ask them to find a quiet place or go for a walk, read the prayers and talk to God about them.

b. Sharing prayer: After a quiet time invite the teens and adults to choose a partner and share with that partner some of the thoughts each has had. Be certain all adults are partners with youth, if possible.

c. After sharing by couples, ask the whole group to assemble and invite individuals to share their thoughts and insights with one another. Encourage people to pray aloud and to ask the group to pray for their intentions.

d. Structure a prayer service during the weekend, one in which some of the Old Testament prayers appear as readings. After the readings always provide a time for reflection. Play music or recordings to set the tone.

2. **Ideas for community building**

The amount of time necessary for this component of the weekend will vary. If the group knows one another, there will be little necessity to spend time on introductions. If, however, some of the members are strangers, be sure to provide adequate time for the group to jell and become unified.

a. Name Tags: Provide the teens and adults with a large (8 x 5) card. Ask them to write their names in large letters in the center. On the upper left hand corner ask them to write the name of the person they consider their greatest hero. In the lower left hand corner, ask them to write the person in the Old Testament they like the most. In the upper right hand corner ask them to put their favorite school subject. In the last corner ask them to put the name of their favorite food.

Invite them to decorate the card and provide crayons, paints and magic markers for this purpose. Once the name tags are complete have them pin them on and spend 15 minutes in silence going from one to the other and talking in sign language with each other as best they can. Break the ban on conversation and allow 15 minutes for conversation.

b. Provide each member of the group with a dozen pipe cleaners. Ask each person to make something with the pipe cleaners which tells about himself/herself. Ask them to share in groups of four and then have each group of four choose one of its members to share with the whole group.

c. Divide the group into pairs. On the board or on newsprint write the following questions: 1) What makes you happy? 2) What makes you sad? 3) What do you like about the Old Testament? Have each pair ask each other these questions until you yell, "Switch" at which point everyone gets a new partner and begins again. Continue the process until the group seems relaxed.

d. Music is the single greatest community builder. Invite students to bring along guitars or other instruments if any of them are proficient. If not, try to find an adult or young adult who will come with the group and invite it to sing several times during the weekend. Most of the songs customarily sung at folk Masses are appropriate. Secular songs are also appropriate as community builders.

3. **Ideas for Instruction**

The Mini Lesson Plans sections with their lists of filmstrips and instructional projects should provide many ideas for the weekend.

The best idea, however, for at least one of the meetings is a simple talk by an adult or teen about his or her own faith and life of prayer. This adult may be the parish priest, the DRE, or other person in the parish. A young college person who is making the weekend may also be asked.

How to schedule the retreat

Most directors of teenager groups find that if they begin early in the evening and run their program well into the night, they take advantage of the best time, although this is difficult for the adults. With a good late sleep, the group can begin again about 11 a.m. and finish just before lunch. Under these circumstances a schedule might go something like this:

5:00	Depart for the retreat center
6:00	Supper clean-up
7:00	Opening mixers (community builders)
7:30	Quiet time for prayer—prayer sharing
8:00	Instruction (talk, filmstrip etc.)
9:00	Project—collage building, something from Mini Lesson Plans, etc.
10:00	Coke and cookies
10:30	Prayer service
11:00	Instruction
11:30	Quiet time for prayer
12:00	Retire
11:00	Morning prayer (Use some of the prayer suggestions in the lessons.)
11:15	Instruction
12:00	Quiet time for prayer
12:30	Lunch
1:30	Depart for the school or parish

Where can we get other ideas?

If the suggestions given here do not fit the needs of your group the following books provide excellent sources of information:

1. *Parish Youth Ministry: A Manual for Beginners in the Art* by Bill and Patty Coleman, (Twenty-Third Publications, P.O. Box 180, West Mystic, CT 06388) has a special section on youth retreats. It is also filled with creative ideas for other forms of youth ministry.

2. *Retreat Resources* by Maury Smith, OFM, (Paulist Press, 545 Island Road, Ramsey, NJ 07466) is a series of three large volumes on retreat planning. The third volume of this series subtitled *Retreats for Youth* will be especially helpful.

3. *Serendipity* is a series of group activity books by Lyman Coleman (Word Publications, 4600 West Waco Drive, Waco, TX 76703). These books contain many impressive suggestions for process education. Some can be easily adapted to retreat use.

About the Authors

William and Patricia Coleman have now written ten revised volumes of the *Mine Is The Morning* high school series. They have also composed an eight-volume series entitled *Daybreak* for religious education at the junior high level and a single-volume manual for youth ministers and teachers entitled *Youth Ministry (A Manual for Beginners in the Art)*. William has authored two filmstrip programs: *Sin and Reconciliation* and *The Mass* and two multi-media adult programs: *The Contemporary Way of the Cross* and *Prayer*.

Patricia holds a degree in communication theory and William a doctorate in adult education. Both are members of Growth Associates, a group of creative people dedicated to sharing the gospel. They are available for workshops and talks.

Credits for this volume:

Cover—Elisabeth Seriki
Page 16—Turkish Tourism & Information Office
Page 20—Editions du Chalet
Page 23—Maryann Read
Page 32—Alan Oddie
Page 36—Egyptian State Tourist Administration
Page 47—Editions du Chalet
Page 48—Editions du Chalet
Page 50—Egyptian State Tourist Administration
Page 52—Paul Schrock
Page 55—Turkish Tourism & Information Office
Page 64—Paul Schrock
Page 71—The Genesis Project
Page 79—The Genesis Project
Page 80—Turkish Tourism & Information Office
Page 84—Turkish Tourism & Information Office
Page 96—Ethiopian Airlines
Page 109—The Photogroup
Page 110—Ethiopian Airlines
Page 114—The Photogroup
Page 117—Mary Lou Rose
Page 125—Swedish National Tourist Office
Page 140—Yale Univ. Art Gallery, New Haven
Page 144—Editions du Chalet
Page 155—Christopher Baldwin

Uncredited Photos—Twenty-Third Archives

Graphics, layout and design by Maryann Read
Printed in the United States of America by Abbey Press, St. Meinrad, Indiana.

Please send and bill me for the books of the Mine Is The Morning program (including duplicator master packets) which I have checked below:

- [ ] The Church: Beginnings and History
- [ ] Personal Morality and the Saints
- [ ] The Beatitudes Today
- [ ] Jesus: His Basic Teachings
- [ ] Jesus: His Parables, Death and Resurrection
- [ ] The Mass and Prayer
- [ ] Sacraments of Service
- [ ] Sacraments of Healing
- [ ] Sexuality and Marriage
- [ ] The Old Testament

Twenty-Third Publications
P. O. Box 180
West Mystic, CT 06388

Single books with master packets: $14.95 each
Complete set (all books and packets): $139.50

Parish _____

Ordered by _____

Address _____

City, State _____ Zip _____